MANIFEST DESTINY

Choosing a Life of Greatness

Stephen Palmer

For ordering information or special discounts for bulk purchases, please contact Stephen Palmer at www.StephenDPalmer.com.

Cover and interior layout designed by Haven Simmons.

Published by Inspiring Greatness, LLC.

www.StephenDPalmer.com

Library of Congress Cataloging-in-Publication Data

Palmer, Stephen
Manifest destiny: choosing a life of greatness / by Stephen Palmer.
ISBN: 978-0-9907339-3-5
Library of Congress Control Number: 2015954249

MANIFEST DESTINY

Choosing a Life of Greatness

AUTHOR'S NOTE

Do you, like me, feel compelled to live a life of excellence and significance, yet struggle daily with personal demons? Do you feel called to some great purpose, yet wonder what it is, exactly?

This book is for you.

Every week I stare at a blank page and do my best to hack out something meaningful and memorable for my "Inspiration Weekly" newsletter subscribers. Some weeks (very few, truthfully) it flows as if heaven is speaking through me. Other weeks I smack into brick wall after brick wall, and it is only with the greatest effort that something worth sharing emerges from the rubble. And *every* week, I feel discouraged by how painfully feeble my attempts are at living the ideals to which I aspire and which I urge my readers to live.

I suppose that's an apt metaphor for all our lives. In our sincerest moments, we feel that deep, inner call, that yearning to be someone worth remembering. We know who we are, what we were born for. Some days we nail it. Other days, well, thank God for repentance and forgiveness. And always, no matter how high we soar, we're painfully aware of how far short we fall of the ideal.

But when we stick with it, and never give up to the trials or give in to the darkness, we can look back at the net result of our lives and see something to be proud of.

After a year of never giving in to the terror of a blank page week after week, I look back and see a body of work I'm proud of. I hope my pride does not exceed your epiphanies as you read it.

In Longfellow's classic poem, "A Psalm of Life," we read,

> *Lives of great men all remind us*
> *We can make our lives sublime,*
> *And, departing, leave behind us*
> *Footprints on the sands of time;*
>
> *Footprints, that perhaps another,*
> *Sailing o'er life's solemn main,*
> *A forlorn and shipwrecked brother,*
> *Seeing, shall take heart again.*

My earnest wish is that this book may be such a footprint for you, and inspire you to take heart in making your life sublime.

Stephen S Palmer

Stephen Palmer

P.S. If you find anything worthwhile in these pages, I invite you to subscribe to my "Inspiration Weekly" newsletter at StephenDPalmer.com to get messages like these every Monday morning.

CONTENTS

To my loyal "Inspiration Weekly" readers, without whom this book would not exist. You make it a pleasure to write.

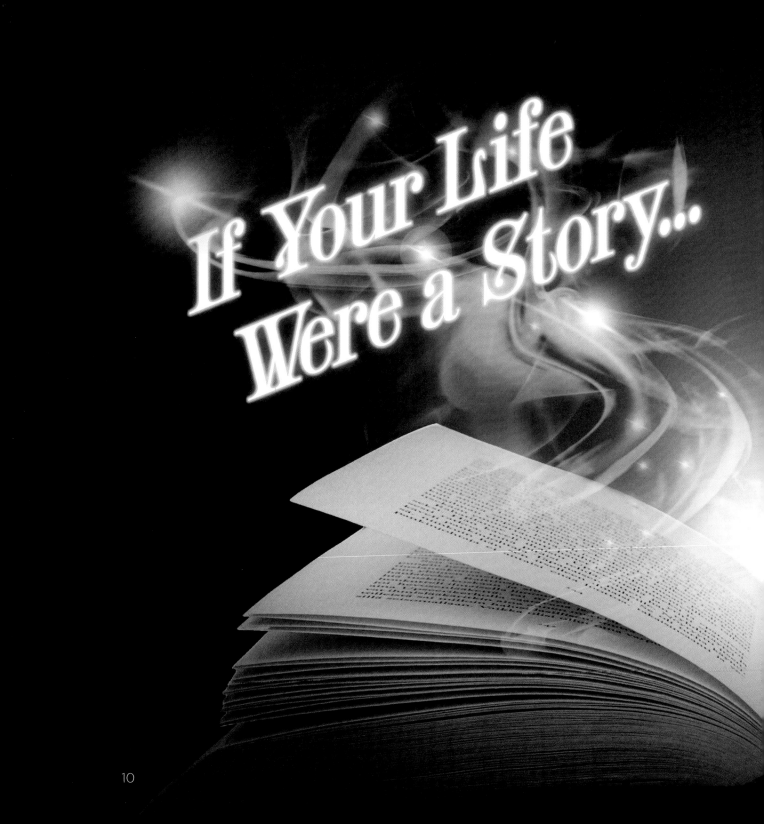

If Your Life Were a Story...

...would your readers be mesmerized as they tore through the pages, or would they toss it aside?

Would they trumpet it to everyone they knew, leaning forward with wide eyes? Or would they forget about it?

Would it shatter chains of fear and doubt and awaken faith and courage? Or would it weary readers with standard routines, pitiful clichés, and plain pettiness?

Would it wallow in normalcy, or soar with inspiration?

Would your readers want to be like you?

How would people feel after reading your story?

Would you be a hero, a villain, or a faceless nobody drowning in a sea of faceless nobodies?

Would your story be told a hundred years after you had passed on?

Would it matter if your story was told or not?

YOUR LIFE *IS* A STORY.

And you're writing it every moment of every day.

IS IT WORTH READING?

CAUGHT IN THE ACT

To manifest a better life, we must first envision a better life.

The word "manifest," defined today as "to make clear or evident to the eye or the understanding," has a fascinating origin. The literal definition of the original word was "caught in the act."

The Latin root *manus*, meaning hand, seems symbolic of man using hands for conscious actions, or making choices. Its accompanying root *festus*, meaning "able to be seized or handled," suggest thoughts made real and concrete.

In other words, that which is manifested can be felt, touched, realized as tangible. Thus, **to manifest is to reveal one's true thoughts, desires, and character through action.** It is to be "caught in the act" of who we are.

Of course, this applies to both improvement and degeneration. One can be caught in the act of anonymous service, or caught in the act of adultery.

No matter where or how we're caught in action, understand that no action can be taken without forming first as a thought. As Plutarch wrote, "An idea is a being incorporeal, which has no subsistence by itself, but gives figure and form unto shapeless matter, and becomes the cause of manifestation."

The Proverb states it more succinctly: "As a man thinketh, so is he..."

What we do is a manifestation of what we think. To manifest a better life, we must first envision a better life. In other words, we need a clear, concrete, and compelling manifesto of our ideal life. A bold declaration of our noblest ideals and highest aspirations, which saturates our thoughts and leads to the manifestation of heroic actions.

Without such a conscious guide, we will manifest the programmed, contradictory, and limiting junk of our subconscious mind. We will be caught in the act of operating on autopilot: blindly accepting social programming, submitting to false labels, believing negative self-talk, accepting unquestioningly what is "known" to be impossible.

To manifest is to reveal one's true thoughts, desires, and character through action.

By default, every human being is a manifester—whether consciously or unconsciously. If we're going to manifest anyway, why not manifest consciously and positively? Knowing thoughts manifest as actions, why entertain limiting and degenerate thoughts?

Eternal vigilance, taught the American Founders, is the price of liberty. This principle is as true for personal liberty as it is true of political and economic freedom. As we think, so shall we become.

We must guard our thoughts vigilantly, for they will manifest as either tragic or triumphant actions. As James Allen wrote in his classic *As a Man Thinketh*,

> *"Mind is the Master power that moulds and makes,*
> *And Man is Mind, and evermore he takes*
> *The tool of Thought, and, shaping what he wills,*
> *Brings forth a thousand joys, a thousand ills:*
> *He thinks in secret, and it comes to pass:*
> *Environment is but his looking-glass."*

Every moment of every day you are caught in the act of manifesting your thoughts. Will you feel embarrassed or excited, guilty or honorable to be caught in action?

TINY BOAT
on a
FATHOMLESS OCEAN

We are pawns in a game
whose forces we largely fail
to comprehend

—Dan Ariely

You are a tiny boat hurled by waves, swirled by winds on a fathomless ocean.

There are monsters in the deep, circling ominously. Spasmodic swells threaten to capsize you. At times you drift drowsily through doldrums. You panic when you lose your bearings in thick fog.

The ocean is your subconscious mind, the boat your conscious mind.

According to Harvard professor Gerald Zaltman, 95 percent of our thoughts, emotions, and learning occur without our conscious awareness. Most cognitive neuroscientists concur. NeuroFocus founder Dr. A.K. Pradeep estimates it at 99.999 percent.

15

Dan Ariely, professor of psychology and behavioral economics at Duke University and author of *Predictably Irrational: The Hidden Forces that Shape Our Decisions*, concludes from years of empirical research that: "We are pawns in a game whose forces we largely fail to comprehend."

David Eagleman, neuroscientist at Baylor College of Medicine and author of *Incognito: The Secret Lives of the Brain*, writes: "Consciousness is the smallest player in the operations of the brain. Our brains run mostly on autopilot, and the conscious mind has little access to the giant and mysterious factory that runs below it."

Dr. Richard Grant of the University of Texas explains that our relationship with our subconscious mind is the same as that with water: We can periodically and briefly swim underneath the surface and discover a hidden fantasy world shimmering with dazzling colors and sensational creatures. But if we spend too much time below, we'll either drown or be devoured by the monsters in the deep.

Like most people, you can toss helplessly on the ocean of subconsciousness—enslaved by unexamined and deeply embedded beliefs, a puppet on the strings of unconscious reaction. Or you can harness the power of the ocean to your advantage.

There's *one* way to survive on the ocean and sail unwaveringly to destinations of your choosing: Use vision to create a fixed, immovable point that acts as your North Star. Then use the rudder and sails of conscious choice to navigate to your fixed point, no matter how colossal the waves and furious the winds.

Take refreshing dips in the ocean through playful imagination. Fish for fresh ideas through introspective meditation.

Be fiercely vigilant about the thoughts you entertain in your conscious mind and the habits you create.

Indulging in unworthy and negative thoughts and addictive behaviors are like flinging blood in the water—the sharks will streak to your boat and tear you to pieces.

Life Manifestos (LifeManifestos.com) are sweet water and fresh food to thirsty and hungry sailors. A cool breeze on a stiflingly hot day on the ocean. They give your conscious mind the nourishment you need to man the rudder and adjust the sails. They give you the strength you need to fight the swarming monsters of temptation, depression, and negative self-talk. They give you the refreshment you need to stay energized through the doldrums. They gleam through night clouds to keep you ever focused on your North Star.

You are a tiny boat on a wild ocean.
But you have the rudders and sails of conscious choice.

Are you using them?

SIX
INESCAPABLE
LAWS OF HABITS

Pioneer wagon wheels cut eternal ruts in plains and rocks across the American west. Likewise, our habits forge irreversible patterns in our brain as we migrate toward our eternal destiny.

Free will comes with the shackles of consequence. Choose our actions we may, but consequences are unavoidable and non-negotiable. And no consequential shackles are as unyielding and unforgiving as the power of habit.

Charles Duhigg's life-changing book, *The Power of Habit: Why We Do What We Do in Life and Business*, details the science behind how habits form and how to change them, including the following six inescapable laws:

LAW #1 | **HABITS CAN NEVER BE ERADICATED**

Close to the center of our skull lies a golf ball-sized lump of tissue called the basal ganglia. Our basal ganglia is the western plains under our wagon wheels of habit. Its job is to store habits even while the rest of our brain goes to sleep.

Science has proven that repeated habits become ingrained into our basal ganglia forever. Our brain is programmed to constantly find new ways to save effort.

Forming habits is one primary way our brains do this. As Duhigg explains, the brain uses a three-step loop to form habits consisting of **cues**, **routines**, and **rewards**. Cues are triggers that prompt your brain to go into automatic mode and tell it which habit routine to launch, e.g. drinking coffee upon waking, putting on your seat belt, etc. Rewards tell your brain whether particular loops are worth remembering for the future.

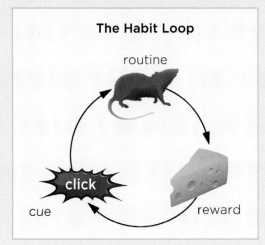

The Habit Loop

routine

click

cue

reward

"Over time," writes Duhigg, "this loop–cue, routine, reward; cue, routine, reward–becomes more and more automatic. The cue and reward become intertwined until a powerful sense of anticipation and craving emerges. Eventually...a habit is born."

Once born, no habit will ever die. As MIT scientist Ann Graybiel says, "Habits never really disappear. They're encoded into the structures of our brain, and that's a huge advantage for us, because it would be awful if we had to relearn how to drive after every vacation."

"The problem is that your brain can't tell the difference between bad and good habits, and so if you have a bad one, it's always lurking there, waiting for the right cues and rewards."

LAW #2 | HABITS ERODE FREE WILL

If this paragraph doesn't arrest your attention like a slap to the face, you're not listening:

"When a habit emerges, the brain stops fully participating in decision making. It stops working so hard, or diverts focus to other tasks. So unless you deliberately fight a habit–unless you find new routines–the pattern will unfold automatically."

Understand that this can work to our salvation, or our damnation. There are some choices we only want to make once. Good habits form a life of automatic, programmed goodness and protect us from poor choices in compromising situations.

The longer bad habits operate, the harder they are to break — in fact, the less we even think about breaking them.

LAW #3 | HABITS CAN ONLY CHANGE FORM; TO CHANGE YOUR HABITS, SHIFT YOUR ROUTINE

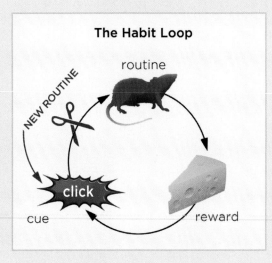

The Habit Loop

routine

NEW ROUTINE

click

cue   reward

Try as we may, for any given habit, the cues and rewards will never change. They are forever hard-wired into our brain. What we can do, however, is change the routine in response to the cue, which leads to the reward.

The trick is to leverage our brain's power of habit in our favor, like Jujitsu, rather than fighting against it with sheer willpower.

We can learn to give our brain the same rewards it perceives from bad habits through new, positive routines. To work, a positive routine shift must actually provide the same level of satisfaction as a bad habit.

LAW #4   HABITS ARE EASIER TO CHANGE WITH A SUPPORT GROUP

Habits, writes Duhigg, cannot be eradicated, but instead can only be replaced. This is achieved by keeping the same cue and the same reward, but inserting a new routine between them.

"But that's not enough," Duhigg cautions. "For a habit to stay changed, people must believe change is possible. And most often, that belief only emerges with the help of a group...

"The evidence is clear: If you want to change a habit, you must find an alternative routine, and your odds of success go up dramatically when you commit to changing as part of a group."

LAW #5   FOCUS ON KEYSTONE HABITS FOR WIDESPREAD CHANGE

"Keystone habits," says Duhigg, are seemingly small and simple habits, but which can catalyze a ripple effect and have a major impact on every aspect of your life.

One such keystone habit is exercise. As Duhigg explains, "When people start habitually exercising, even as infrequently as once a week, they start changing other, unrelated patterns in their lives, often unknowingly. Typically, people who exercise start eating better and becoming more productive at work. They smoke less and show more patience with colleagues and family. They use their credit cards less frequently and say they feel less stressed. It's not completely clear why. But for many people, exercise is a keystone habit that triggers widespread change."

James Prochaska, a researcher at the University of Rhode Island, adds, "Exercise spills over. There's something about it that makes other good habits easier."

LAW #6   WRITE DOWN YOUR PLANS FOR DEALING WITH TEMPTATION & OBSTACLES

Studies have routinely shown that people who anticipate and write down how they will react to temptations and obstacles when striving to overcome a habit are much more successful than those who do not.

Writing our plan down makes us more conscious of our cues, and helps us focus on our rewards. It also strengthens our willpower.

American pioneers, drawn irresistibly by Manifest Destiny, left their mark upon the plains. Our habits will manifest our destiny, and determine the mark we leave. As William James wrote, "All our life is but a mass of habits—practical, emotional, and intellectual—systematically organized for our weal or woe, and bearing us irresistibly toward our destiny..."

I SAW EMBARRASSMENT AND SHAME IN HIS DARTING EYES AND SHUFFLING FEET AS HE ANSWERED.

MY HEART ACHED FOR HIM.

FIFTEEN YEARS AFTER GRADUATING HIGH SCHOOL, I HAD RETURNED TO MY HOMETOWN TO VISIT MY PARENTS, WHERE I ENCOUNTERED AN OLD FRIEND WHOM I HADN'T SEEN SINCE GRADUATION.

As a youth, he had had no confidence. He hadn't changed a bit. To the world–and to himself–he was a downtrodden loser from a no-account family, with no prospects, no ambition, no hope of accomplishing anything meaningful. His life was as broken down as the rusty cars strewn across his family's front yard.

Pleased to see him and to catch up, I asked him, "So what do you do?"

"I'm just a mechanic," he answered apologetically.

The small word "just" revealed significant insights into his soul.

What makes one man embarrassed of his life and another proud and confident? What makes one man strive for greatness and another cower in fear and wallow in hopelessness? One factor: What they believe about themselves.

THE MOST IMPORTANT FACTOR

What you believe about yourself determines your destiny more than any other factor. Your behavior is a product of your beliefs. If you believe you're a loser, you'll act like a loser. Winners believe they are winners long before they accomplish their goals and collect their trophies.

Belief is the starting point of all achievement. You cannot become successful until you believe you are worthy of success. It is impossible to achieve empowering goals while being crippled by limiting beliefs about yourself. Your net worth is largely determined by your self-worth.

You cannot depend on praise and encouragement from others to create a positive self-perception. In fact, you can be certain that the world will try to tear you down. What you believe about yourself must come from within.

To the world, Frederick Douglass was a bastard mulatto slave, a sub-human, chattel to be bought and sold like furniture. But Frederick knew better. As he wrote in his autobiography, "From my earliest recollection, I date the entertainment of a deep conviction that slavery would not always be able to hold me within its foul embrace; and in the darkest hours of my career in slavery, this living word of faith and spirit of hope departed not from me, but remained like ministering angels to cheer me through the gloom."

To the world, Abraham Lincoln was nothing but a poor, uneducated country boy. To the world, Florence Nightingale was "just" a nurse.

What matters isn't what you do, but what you believe about what you do.

Are mechanics dumb, untalented, greasy low-lifes? Or is being a mechanic a noble and honorable profession, a God-given mission to solve problems, make things better, and make people happy?

The answer is not intrinsic to the profession; it is a belief. What a mechanic believes about his profession determines whether he is respected and admired, or ignored and ridiculed. His belief, not his natural talent, determines whether his work is sloppy or excellent. His perception of himself, not the world's, determines whether he is proud or embarrassed of his work.

THAT DETERMINES YOUR DESTINY

If I could do just one thing to transform my friend's life, I wouldn't change his occupation. I wouldn't reform his habits. I wouldn't give him a million dollars. I wouldn't make him famous.

I would look deep into his eyes and sear these truths into his soul: "You are a Son of God. In your veins flows royal blood. The Creator of the universe loves you more than you can comprehend. You are good, noble, and powerful beyond measure. You can achieve anything you believe. You can overcome any obstacle. Nothing you do is insignificant. You were born for greatness."

And from those fundamental beliefs would spring hope, faith, joy, and confidence...

AN INEXCUSABLE DOUBLE STANDARD THAT CRIPPLES LIVES

Desperate for solace and support, your dearest friend comes to you in tears, confessing a common mistake, berating him or herself mercilessly. What do you say?

"Yes, you're absolutely right. You've made a horrible mistake that can never be righted. You will never be forgiven. You are a horrible person. You should be ashamed of yourself."

Your closest friend comes to you drowning in discouragement, on the brink of giving up. What do you say?

"Yes, you should quit now. It's only going to get harder. You're not good enough. You are a loser and you'll never amount to anything. It's pointless to even try. What a joke. What were you thinking anyway?"

Good people are undoubtedly repulsed by those incomprehensible responses. We know that "Your friend is the man who knows all about you, and still likes you," as Elbert Hubbard said. We agree with Henry Brooks Adams that, "Every man should have a fair-sized cemetery in which to bury the faults of his friends." We know a friend is one who believes in us when we have ceased to believe in ourselves.

Then why, oh why, do we talk to ourselves in ways we would never dream of talking to our friends?

Why do we offer comfort, support, and encouragement to our friends in times of dire need, then turn around and torment, criticize, and discourage ourselves? Why do we teach our children to be kind and loving to others, while being harsh and spiteful to ourselves?

25

Negative self-talk is no more acceptable than gossiping about or tearing down others. It's no more true or helpful than what ignorant people would say to criticize our friends. Our immediate reaction to it should be exactly the same as when we catch our children verbally trashing someone.

Longfellow said, "We judge ourselves by what we feel capable of doing, while others judge us by what we have already done." I think he's right in what he *said*, but wrong in what he *meant*. We do judge ourselves by our potential—but not to see ourselves as greater than we are, but rather to beat ourselves up.

Not as in, "I could write a beautiful piece of music. I could write a masterpiece novel. I could create a world-changing business. I am wonderful." But as in, "I could do all those things. But I haven't. I'm worthless."

We learn from sages and proverbs that self-mastery is the ultimate key to achievement and fulfillment.

*"He who rules his spirit has won a
greater victory than the taking of a city."*

—Proverbs 16:32

*"Mastering others is strength;
mastering yourself is true power."*

—Lao Tzu

*"One who conquers himself is greater than another who
conquers a thousand times a thousand men on the battlefield."*

—Buddha

26

But these teachings apply to more than just virtue (e.g. guarding against impure thoughts, avoiding addictions, controlling your responses to harm from others or adverse circumstances, etc.). They also apply to winning the battle against negative self-talk.

We're not just out of integrity when we disparage others, but also when we disparage ourselves. Negative self-talk is an inexcusable, hypocritical double standard. We don't deserve it any more than our dearest friends deserve to be belittled. As Tal Ben-Shahar said: "Why the double standard, the generosity toward our neighbor and the miserliness where we ourselves are concerned? And so I propose that we add a new rule to our moral code: 'Do not do unto yourself what you would not do unto others.'"

And as Goethe said: "Treat people as if they were what they ought to be and you help them to become what they are capable of being."

This applies to how we treat ourselves, too.

Treat yourself as you would treat your dearest friend. Uplift, encourage, and motivate yourself. Be your best coach. Inspire yourself to greatness.

When you make mistakes or feel dejected and discouraged, tell yourself exactly what you would tell your friends.

Eliminate the double standard of negative self-talk in your life and watch yourself soar.

THE TWO
MOST POWERFUL WORDS
KNOWN TO MAN

Kindly remove your shoes, honored reader; we stand on holy ground. Enter this sacred temple. Let us reverently approach the altar.

Do you know the temple of which I speak? Do you detect the magic that gushes through your veins, that permeates your cells, that animates your every act?

Lean in closely. I will whisper the word—the force—that both redeems and damns, that elevates and debases, creates and destroys, that builds men and nations and dashes them to dust.

The temple in which we stand, this altar we approach, the holy ground that sustains humanity, the magic, the power, the word is this: **CHOICE**.

Yours is the choice to fashion dreams or to wallow in the swamp of unrealized potential. Yours is the choice to heal or to abuse. Yours is the choice to take offense or to understand. Yours is the choice to speak with purity or obscenity. Yours is the choice to show compassion or to criticize.

Yours is the choice to avoid choosing, thus banishing yourself to the dungeon of mediocrity.

LISTEN: Choice speaks to those with ears to hear.

You, who trudge through uniform days, entrenched in monotony, embattled with triviality, burdened by pettiness, thwarted by distraction.

To you, Choice urges: *Awake and arise to greatness.*

You, emasculated by entitlement, whose lives are shrunken and hollow from placing blame, whose creativity is consumed devising excuses, whose power is sucked dry by the vacuum of victimhood.

To you, Choice declares: *Embrace responsibility.*

You, whose energy is drained by harbored pain, whose lives revolve around taking offense, who derive twisted pleasure from suffering, whose existence is circumscribed by the actions of others.

To you, Choice fervently whispers: *Surrender thy pain.*

You, consumed by lust, embroiled in unbridled passion, haunted by insatiable craving, stained by sordid pleasure, drowning in filth, driven mad by counterfeits.

To you, Choice warns: *Master thyself.*

You, enraptured by the illusory gleam of steel, held captive by convenience, enticed by shortcuts, suffering from superficiality, whose idol is American Idol, whose highest ideal is retirement, for whom comfort is the defining criterion of the good life.

To you, Choice pleads: *Seek the divine.*

You, plagued by ambition, addicted to power, who sell your soul to control, who abandon principles to manipulate, whose beam-stuffed eyes probe for external slivers.

To you, Choice challenges: *Turn inward.*

You, imprisoned by fear, enlisted in the mob, who tread lightly on the well-beaten path, who leave no mark to follow, who squander your gifts by fitting in, whose truest Self remains unclaimed.

To you, Choice exclaims: *Seize your birthright!*

To humanity this sacred, limitless power shouts from the rooftops: CHOOSE WISELY!

You are no puppet, no ward of the state, no powerless, tepid, spineless creature. You are no mere beast, subject to instinct.

Pierce the veil of your limitations. Shed fear. Cast aside the entrapments of your past life of unconscious enslavement. Shun the demons of doubt as they strive to stifle your Voice.

Reject bitterness and anger. Expel the darkness from your life with love-choices, and no form of negativity, deceit, or degeneracy can withstand your presence.

The essence of darkness, in all its hideous manifestations, is this: You do not have a choice.

Darkness is a miserable, twisted devil hissing in your ear: "You are not good enough. You are not smart enough. You are powerless. Do not even try to become something better—you will get made fun of, you will be hurt, you will only be disappointed by your failure. It is her fault. He made you do it. You are entitled. No one will see."

Command the darkness to flee before you. Strike that demon to the ground. Trample him with the fierceness of creation.

> Choice is your, privilege, your birthright,
> your heritage. Choice is your curse if you fail to exercise
> it to elevate your life and fuel your endeavors.

Will yours be the tragedy of what might have been, or the legacy of what is?

Answer that question not with words, but with deeds. Answer it not by default, but by design.

Carve out your path from the fertile wilderness of the unknown, the untried. Apply your intuition, vision, heart, mind, hand, might, and strength to thought, words, and material. Harness them, shape them, mold them into something different, more useful, more holy. Manifest reality from potential.

Leap into the darkness. If you are not caught, can landing be any worse than your current existence? You will land. And your old, limited, fearful self will shatter into oblivion. Your pure Self will remain, from which you will craft a choiceful life—the only life worth living.

Leverage choice to propel you ever higher, purer, nobler, more capable, more useful.

Exit this temple now, exalted reader, and carry this intense light, this pure knowledge through your sojourn.

This, dear reader, is the freedom you crave.

. . . .

Do you know the "two most powerful words known to man"? No, they do not appear together in this article. Email your guess to me@stephendpalmer.com to get 25 percent off your next purchase at LifeManifestos.com. Guess right and I'll give you a manifesto poster of your choice.

HEROES' RESPONSES TO
DAMNING "SCIENTIFIC EVIDENCE"

"Gathering evidence from both psychology and the neurosciences has provided convincing support for the idea that free will is an illusion." So says Raj Raghunathan, Ph.D. on www.psychologytoday.com.

Decades earlier, while imprisoned in a Nazi concentration camp, Viktor Frankl scratched a tedious response on hoarded scraps of paper, which would eventually be pieced together as one of the most important books in the history of the world, *Man's Search for Meaning*:

> *"What about human liberty? Is there no spiritual freedom in regard to behavior and reaction to any given surroundings? Is that theory true which would have us believe that man is no more than a product of many conditional and environmental factors—be they of a biological, psychological, or sociological nature? Is man but an accidental product of these?*

> *"Most important, do the prisoners' reactions to the singular world of the concentration camp prove that man cannot escape the influences of his surroundings? Does man have no choice of action in the face of such circumstances?*

> *"We can answer these questions from experience as well as on principle. The experiences of camp life show that man does have a choice of action.*

> *"There were enough examples, often of a heroic nature, which proved that apathy could be overcome, irritability suppressed. Man can preserve a vestige of spiritual freedom, of independence of mind, even in such terrible conditions of psychic and physical stress.*

> *"We who lived in the concentration camps can remember the men who walked through the huts comforting others, giving away their last piece of bread.*

> *"They may have been few in number, but they offer sufficient proof that **everything can be taken away from a man but one thing: the last of the human freedoms— to choose one's attitude in any given set of circumstances, to choose one's own way."***

Another concentration camp survivor, Corrie ten Boom, offered her response soon after World War II. After speaking on love and forgiveness at a church service in Munich, Germany, she was approached by the S.S. officer who had stood guard at the shower room door of her concentration camp.

"How grateful I am for your message, Fraulein," he said. "To think that, as you say, He has washed my sins away."

As her previous tormentor extended his hand, Corrie was flooded with memories of standing naked before cruel and mocking men, of her sister dying in camp.

"As I took his hand," she wrote in *The Hiding Place*, "the most incredible thing happened. From my shoulder to my arm and through my hand a current seemed to pass from me to him, while into my heart sprang a love for this stranger that almost overwhelmed me."

Jacques Lusseyran, blind leader of the French Resistance to the Nazis, wrote his response in his transcendently beautiful book, *And There Was Light*, after being imprisoned in Buchenwald for two years: "This is what you had to do to live in the camp: be engaged, not live for yourself alone. The self-centered life has not place in the world of the deported...Be engaged, no matter how, but be engaged...

"Joy I found even in strange byways, in the midst of fear itself. And fear departed from me, as infection leaves an abscess when it bursts."

Frederick Douglass, Booker T. Washington, Louis Zamparelli, Immaculee Ilibagiza, The Van Nguyen, Nick Vujicic and others have also responded with their lives.

These heroes are not the exception. Rather, their actions prove the rule and provide the standard for all humanity.

ONE PERSON CHOOSING FORGIVENESS OVER BITTERNESS
PROVES THAT ANYONE CAN FORGIVE.
ONE PERSON CHOOSING MEANING AND PURPOSE
OVER APATHY PROVES THAT ANYONE CAN.

One hero exercising the power of choice to transcend circumstances leaves the rest of us with no excuse, with an example to emulate, a possibility to strive for.

As George Roche wrote in *A World Without Heroes*, "The anti-hero dismisses all purpose as illusion. It sees us as helpless pawns, unable to act or even think on our own, fully shaped and determined by outside forces. It reaches this position with tortuous chains of inference, with misused 'scientific assumptions' and fanciful formulas that dare to tell us what we can and cannot know, what is and is not real.

"But this is all contrivance, serving not the search for knowledge and truth, but the rebel's own dark purposes.

"And it is all belied in an instant by that one purposeful, death-defying act or a hero. That act, a reality known to us all, tells us more about the human condition than all of the empty and life-hating mutterings of modernist philosophers. It serves a Good we all may turn to for fulfillment in our lives."

IRREFUTABLE EXPERIENTIAL EVIDENCE FROM THE
BIOGRAPHIES OF MANKIND'S GREATEST HEROES
PROVE THAT WE HAVE THE POWER TO CHOOSE. AND
WITH THAT POWER, WE CAN TRANSCEND THE MOST
HORRIFIC CIRCUMSTANCES.

NO MATTER WHAT HAPPENS TO US, NO MATTER
OUR BIRTH OR PAST, NO MATTER OUR LIMITATIONS,
WE CAN CHOOSE TO BE HAPPY, LOVING,
PRODUCTIVE, HEROIC, AND FREE.

WE ARE BEST FRIENDS. In our home you are loved — wanted, appreciated, and cherished—no matter what. You are safe to be vulnerable. To be silly. To vent your frustrations. To share your emotions, struggles, and embarrassments. We encourage you to ◆ We give you confidence to dream BIG, WE ARE Family ◆ venture into the world and we do everything and get knocked possible to make your dreams come true. down. Come back to us.

◆ WE COMFORT, HEAL, AND STRENGTHEN YOU. ◆ And whisk you back out the door with a smile on your face, the dream glistening in your eyes, courage beating in your heart. ◆ WE BELIEVE We're on your team. In your corner. in you. Your biggest fans. Cheering our hearts out for you to reach, strive, leave it all on the field, become who you were born to become. We are family: united, unbreakable, eternal.

Available for purchase as a 16 x 20 poster or canvas print at LifeManifestos.com.

WHY THE FAMILY MANIFESTO ALMOST GOT HIJACKED BY THE PAST

"I choose to rise above my past, my pain, my limiting beliefs."

WRITING THE 143-WORD FAMILY MANIFESTO TOOK ME THREE AGONIZING WEEKS AND PLUNGED ME INTO A DEEP DEPRESSION.

You see, the fervent ideal expressed in the manifesto is far removed from the harsh reality I experienced.

Day after grievous day, I stared at the blank page. Night after awful night, I stared at the ceiling. Casting for fresh ideas only dredged up painful memories. I've been a professional freelance writer for seven years. I don't get writer's block. But blocked I was. Mired in misery. Gripped by gloom. Saturated with cynicism.

A rudimentary draft was stitched together, then quickly discarded. At one point I typed disgustedly, "Family is where you get hurt the most," turned off my computer, and escaped my office.

I returned the next day, hanging by a thread through grim determination and aggressive self-therapy.

The breakthrough came when I shifted from thinking about my personal experience to envisioning the safe environment I desperately crave to create for my children. I pictured each of my four angelic children. *What do you ache for them to know to their bones*, I thought.

And the sun burst through the clouds and the manifesto poured from my soul within minutes. Only one word was changed afterwards from the original.

I suspect that many people who have purchased the manifesto had a similar experience to mine. And like me, your deepest desire is to break the cycle and ensure the opposite experience for your children.

And despite your desire, and also like me, I suspect there are times when you fall short of your ideal in how you treat your spouse and children.

And therein lies the power of a prominently displayed manifesto: it is our constant reminder to do, be, and live better.

The more we and our families read it, the more it permeates our subconscious, influences our speech and actions, stretches our vision, purifies our desires. It is a beacon of hope through storms of emotional turmoil.

An idealistic manifesto is not ignorant of excruciating realities. It is not a naïve and fanciful expression of lofty intangibles. It is a gritty, gutsy proclamation grounded in the recognition of disturbing imperfection, yet driven by the certain knowledge that progression is possible through choice.

As William James wrote, "The greatest discovery of my generation is that a human being can alter his life by altering his attitude."

A manifesto is one's planted flag declaring:

- **I CHOOSE to rise above my past, my pain, my limiting beliefs.**
- **I CHOOSE to drag myself from the canvas every time I'm knocked down.**
- **I CHOOSE to never give up striving for the ideal.**
- **I CHOOSE to live from the space between stimulus and response.**
- **I CHOOSE to live from a vision of joy, rather than wounds from the past.**
- **I CHOOSE to be governed by love rather than pain.**
- **I CHOOSE to be a victor, not a victim.**

The Family Manifesto—and the whole idea of Life Manifestos (LifeManifestos.com)— almost died. But it lives. Because I made a choice.

HOW THE LIMITATIONS OF CHOICE SET US

FREE

FOR EIGHT AGONIZING YEARS, NICK VUJICIC PLEADED WITH GOD, "WHY? WHY WAS I BORN THIS WAY? I DON'T UNDERSTAND HOW YOU CAN SAY YOU LOVE ME WHEN YOU ALLOW ME TO STAY IN THIS PAIN."

THE ANSWER FINALLY CAME TO HIM THROUGH THE SCRIPTURE VERSES JOHN 9:1-3.

WHEN HE READ, "…THAT THE WORKS OF GOD SHOULD BE MADE MANIFEST IN HIM," NICK UNDERSTOOD WHY HE WAS BORN WITH NO ARMS OR LEGS (*LIFEWITHOUTLIMBS.ORG*). WITH THAT UNDERSTANDING, HE CHOSE TO LIVE NOT AS A VICTIM, BUT AS A VICTOR, AND OPPORTUNITIES PREVIOUSLY UNSEEN EMERGED.

From the beginning of time, man has questioned whether he is truly in control of his destiny, or if he is merely an insignificant pawn in a game over which he has no control. The vast and unfathomable forces beyond our control—from our DNA and physical characteristics to the family, country, and circumstances we were born in; from the people we meet to the educational opportunities we're exposed to; from the cultural perspectives we're immersed in from birth to natural disasters—seem so overwhelming as to render the power of choice simplistic and virtually meaningless.

But we have ultimate control over two things
that trump all uncontrollable forces combined:
OUR ATTITUDES AND OUR ACTIONS.

Each of us has been dealt a hand. We cannot control the cards we were given, but only how we play them. We cannot control what happens to us, but we *can* control how we respond.

Ironically, it's when we understand and accept the limitations of choice that its true power is unleashed. By accepting what we cannot control, we're empowered to focus on what we can control.

We cannot will our way—pushing through forces beyond our control—to success. But we can create the right conditions that lead to success. Our goals are achieved less by pursuing them directly, and more by cultivating the right conditions for them to manifest as a natural byproduct. As John Maxwell says, "Small disciplines repeated with consistency every day lead to great achievements gained slowly over time."

Salesmen can't control whether or not a prospect will buy. But they can control how much they know about their product. They can study and learn persuasion techniques. They can control how many people they contact, and whether or not they give up.

Writers can't control how their content is received. But they can control how much they write.

We can't control genetic predispositions toward disease or addiction. But we can control how we eat and live.

We can't control what accidents may befall us. But we can prepare to respond with faith and hope by practicing spiritual disciplines daily, such as prayer, meditation, and studying spiritual texts.

We can't control the choices our children will make. But we can control how we treat them and the environment we create for them.

We stumble over uncontrollable blocks every day. But it is precisely by recognizing that we have no control over them that we transform them into stepping stones. Our lives are transformed, our destinies realized as we accept what we cannot control and focus on what we can control.

WE CAN'T CONTROL HOW WE WERE BORN.
BUT WE CAN CONTROL HOW WE LIVE.

A
SUCCESS SECRET
REVEALED BY A
Quality Woman

43

As my amazing wife, Queen Karina, and our kids prepared for their weekly trip to the library, they discovered they were missing several borrowed CDs. They ransacked the house for several hours. Nothing turned up.

She took them to the library, where she was informed that the CDs would cost $100 to replace. She came home and never said a word about it to me. She gathered the children, they crafted a plan.

I came out of my home office for lunch and found her making kettle corn. She said I couldn't eat any because it was for a project. I thought nothing of it, finished my lunch, and resumed work.

Late that afternoon she arrived home with the children and announced they had earned $5.

"$5 for what?" I asked.

"To pay back our $100 library fee," she explained.

She had divided the kettle corn into small paper bags and had taken our children with her to sell them door-to-door in our neighborhood for fifty cents a bag. And I fell in love all over again. They were still at it, selling baked goods door-to-door, a week later.

Here's the thing: We didn't need the money. We were doing just fine. Such a hefty library fee is annoying, to be sure. There are plenty of other things we'd rather spend $100 on. But she could have just paid the fine from our checking account and moved on.

But she stepped up and took responsibility—and in the process taught our children invaluable lessons that I will ensure they remember forever. No pride. No whining. No finger-pointing. No wasting energy looking back. No spreading of negative energy from the frustration.

That, my friend, is a quality woman. A damn fine woman, if you don't mind my saying so. A woman that makes me want to be a better man. A woman to walk and work with side-by-side through eternity.

There are plenty of universal lessons to be drawn from this story: how to be a producer, how to teach children responsibility, how to respond to setbacks, how your example in seemingly insignificant moments makes a profound difference, etc.

But here's the lesson I want to focus on: We can read hundreds of books about living with intention, excellence, and inspiration. We can study and apply the science of harnessing subconscious power to achieve goals. We can stuff our heads full of content on vision, integrity, tenacity, goal-setting and planning, following our bliss.

But the way we cultivate our relationships with our spouses determines our success far more than any of those things combined.

After twenty years of research spanning 2,000 years of history and analyzing hundreds of the most successful men, in *Think and Grow Rich* Napoleon Hill detailed the common threads he discovered that led to their success. Among other principles, he discovered that, "The pages of history are filled with the records of great leaders whose achievements may be traced directly to the influence of women who aroused the creative faculties of their minds...

"...every great leader, whom [Hill] had the privilege of analyzing, was a man whose achievements were largely inspired by a woman..."

Of course, this applies to great women being inspired by quality husbands as well.

Now here's the real lesson: You want a spouse that still makes you weak in the knees, proud in the heart, and watery in the eyes after fifty years of marriage? A quality spouse who makes you fall head-over-heels in love daily?

Be that kind of a spouse. Like my Queen is to me.

WHY FAILING HARDER
HELPS US SUCCEED FASTER

You remember of course, the wildly successful "The Man Your Man Could Smell Like" Old Spice ads ("I'm on a horse.").

You may not know, however, the radical philosophy that spawned them. The ads were created by Wieden+Kennedy, one of the most innovative and successful ad agencies in the world.

On a wall of their headquarters in the Pearl District of Portland, Oregon hangs a huge white canvas filled with tens of thousands of clear plastic pushpins. It's only by stepping away from the pushpin mural that the slogan appears: <u>Fail Harder</u>.

As an abject failure myself, I'm enamored with the motto. I love a good failure, and I have the greatest respect for people who fail frequently and productively. I have little respect for people who fail from a lack of trying, and I steer clear of those who fail often but never seem to learn the right lessons.

Productive failure is the fastest and most valuable school — provided you have the right attitude. As Henry Ford said, "Failure is only the opportunity to more intelligently begin again." The key is to actually begin anew, savvier, tougher, and even more enthusiastic. Few people do. **The school of hard knocks provides little education to those who focus more on their bruises than on jumping off the mat.**

Just ask Winston Churchill—a master of productive failure. Said he, "Success is stumbling from failure to failure with no loss of enthusiasm." He also said, "Success is not final, failure is not fatal: it is the courage to continue that counts."

If all you learn from failure is that you shouldn't have done the thing that failed, well, you've flunked out of the school of failure. There's a big red "F" slashed through your report card. You can pack your bags and join the ranks of the armchair criticizers—materially comfortable and spiritually miserable.

As Elbert Hubbard said, "The greatest mistake a person can make is to be afraid of making one." Wayne Gretzky adds, "You'll always miss 100 percent of the shots you don't take."

The committed innovator *aspires* to failure. Every successful person has earned a Ph.D. in failure.

Talk-show host Sally Jesse Raphael couldn't pay her credit card bill for twenty-six years. She moved twenty-five times looking for work. She was fired eighteen times. She worked for twenty-six years before she earned an annual salary of $22,000, and she suffered through periods of living on food stamps and sleeping in her car.

Jack Canfield and Mark Victor Hansen submitted their *Chicken Soup for the Soul* manuscript to thirty-three publishers before finally being accepted by number thirty-four. They've since sold more than 100 million copies.

Roy H. Williams reveals, "Follow a trail of bold mistakes and at the end of them you will find a genius."

Frequent failure means you're trying hard. If you try hard enough for long enough—and learn the right lessons from your failures—success is inevitable.

As Thomas J. Watson says, "Would you like me to give you a formula for success? It's quite simple. Double your rate of failure."

Adversity and failure will overtake you at some point in your life no matter what you do. Why not ride out to meet them, fight your battles, and get it over with so you can enjoy success sooner? The more you try to escape adversity and failure, the slower your path to success.

Napoleon Hill said, "Every adversity carries with it the seed of an equivalent or greater benefit." But you can't cultivate those seeds and harvest the benefits if all you focus on is the pain of failure.

Benjamin Franklin said, "The things which hurt, instruct." The challenge is to learn the right lessons from the things which hurt. Are you learning from your failures to stop trying, or are you learning how to try more effectively the next time? Are you getting smarter, or simply more wounded, tired, and jaded?

Look at yourself. Now look at the person you know you could be. Now look back at yourself.

Sadly, the person you could be is not you. But if you started failing harder and smarter, you could become that person.

Anything is possible when you fail hard and learn fast.
So get back up on the horse...

LIFE LESSONS FROM A "GARBAGE SEX SYMBOL"

"If they was to put a garbage man in the Guinness World Book of Records, I would be in there,"

One of my greatest heroes is Revolutionary War general, first American President, and Founding Father George Washington.

And right up with him is New Orleans garbage man Cornelius Washington. Dubbing him the "wizard of trash cans," the New Orleans Times-Picayune published a tribute for him when he died in 2008:

Washington's street choreography of playful twirling and tossing often prompted applause.

With a full trash can in each arm, he would "pop" both cans upside-down into the truck's metal jaws, then set them back on the curb without losing his stride.

From seemingly impossible distances, he would toss dozens of bags and boxes rapid-fire, landing them all in the back of the truck without dropping a scrap of paper.

"Cornelius was amazing. He could do things that I didn't think that people could do with garbage," said Dorothy Taylor, who has driven New Orleans garbage trucks for 18 years. She added, "He would take one route and do it by himself. He was like two men in one. No machine could beat him. No man could beat him. If he was tired, you'd never know it. "He was like a garbage sex symbol."

...Washington said hoppers in other cities seemed lackluster. "It's too textbook," he said. "They stop the truck. They step off the truck. They pick up the can. They dump it. Then they put the can back down in that one spot."

No comparison with New Orleans, where hoppers like him had nearly perfected the art of trash pickup, he said.

"If they was to put a garbage man in the Guinness World Book of Records, I would be in there," he said.

His boasting wasn't based on showmanship alone. Washington knew where each handicapped and elderly neighbor lived and taught younger hoppers to return cans right to their doors. He also told them to work together with other hoppers on big stacks of refuse and to warn the truck driver about street closings, children, drunks and careless bicyclists.

"Every driver wanted Cornelius on his truck," Taylor said. "There will never be another like him."

—End

I once had neighbors whose eleven-year-old son was passionate about garbage collecting. Every time I saw him he talked to me about garbage.

Strangely, my neighbors were embarrassed by their son's passion. I was puzzled by their embarrassment; garbage collecting and disposal is a profound service for humanity. I'd be proud and honored if my son turned out like Cornelius Washington. As Martin Luther King, Jr. said, "If a man is called to be a street sweeper, he should sweep the streets even as Michelangelo painted or Beethoven composed music, or Shakespeare wrote poetry. He should sweep streets so well that all the hosts of heaven and earth will pause to say, 'Here lived a great street sweeper who did his job well.'"

Cornelius Washington may not hold a world record, but he holds the light of excellence up to the world. He may not be mentioned in history textbooks, but my children will know he's a hero.

WHAT MY IRKSOME SHOWER DOOR
TEACHES ABOUT LIVING WITH EXCELLENCE

MY SHOWER DOOR IS UPSIDE DOWN. I KNOW THIS BECAUSE THE LABEL, WHICH IS ETCHED INTO THE GLASS, IS ON THE TOP, THE WORDS UPSIDE DOWN. IT IRKS ME SO MUCH I HAVE TO AVERT MY EYES EVERY TIME I SHOWER.

I imagine the worker who installed it, upon discovering he'd put it in upside down, shrugging his shoulders carelessly and thinking, "Meh, no one will ever notice." How he sleeps at night I will never know.

EXCELLENCE HAS NOTHING TO DO WITH WHO ELSE NOTICES. IT IS A FIERCE, UNYIELDING COMMITMENT TO YOURSELF.

A COMMITMENT THAT YOU'LL NEVER CUT CORNERS. THAT YOU REFUSE TO STAND FOR SLOPPY WORK. THAT YOU HOLD YOURSELF TO A HIGHER STANDARD THAN ANYONE ELSE EXPECTS OF YOU.

In fact, it is particularly those times when no one else will ever know that matter most. **A man who compromises privately will never rise to his potential publicly. A man whose standards are determined by the expectations of others can only rise to the level to which others will allow him.**

As Howard Thurman said, "There is something in every one of you that waits and listens for the sound of the genuine in yourself. It is the only true guide you will ever have. And if you cannot hear it, you will all of your life spend your days on the ends of strings that somebody else pulls."

I judge a craftsman—both his work and his heart—by the dusty, concealed nooks and crannies. By the tiny details that reveal tremendous insights into his character.

Furthermore, it makes no difference whether he's a janitor or a CEO.

Excellence can be cultivated in any station in life. Cleaning toilets and digging ditches are honorable work — if one does them with excellence.

And performing with excellence is the guaranteed path to increasing your value to others, and therefore your personal prosperity and fulfillment.

One could say it's just a shower door. I say it's a window into a worker's soul.

FIVE INDISPENSABLE WAYS TO STAY ON TRACK THROUGH LIFE

*I wasn't but a hundred yards into it
when I realized I was in for a serious challenge.
I was scared I wasn't going to make it.*

After I had been swimming regularly for about six months, Queen Karina and I retreated to a bed-and-breakfast on a lake. I looked across the lake and thought, "I could swim that."

I estimated that it was about a half mile across, making for a mile swim, which I had done plenty of times. That is, in an indoor pool. But open water swimming is drastically different than indoor lap swimming—an important fact I didn't realize until that day.

I fought the fear of not being able to see more than two feet in front of me. Every time I came up for air, waves slapped my face, making me choke.

But the hardest challenge was not being able to swim in a straight line. I had fixed my eyes on a large white rock across the lake as my goal. At first I tried taking fifty strokes before checking my progress. But I found that I was veering considerably to either side each time.

The only way I could stay on track was by looking up at my goal and recalibrating as necessary every twenty strokes instead. Thus, my progress was slow and tedious. But without constantly checking my progress, I never would have made it.

All too often, we put our heads down and swim through life without periodically checking to see if we're headed the right way. After years of hard work and largely thoughtless routines, we raise our heads and realize we've been swimming in the wrong direction.

Even the most focused and committed must continually reconnect with their ultimate vision and most meaningful objectives to stay on track.

HOW TO NEVER LOSE SIGHT OF YOUR OBJECTIVES & STAY ON TRACK

FIVE RECOMMENDATIONS

1. DAILY MEDITATION

I learned the power of this habit from one of my mentors, Steve D'Annunzio (SoulPurposeInstitute.com).

This is an incredibly effective way to constantly reconnect with what is most important. It's like coming up for air.

Take fifteen to twenty minutes a day. Push aside distractions. Just be in the moment. Connect with the real you beyond your thoughts.

After doing this consistently for a month or two, you'll be amazed at how calm, peaceful, and focused you become, the clarity you experience, and how many insights you gain.

2. WEEKLY PLANNING

Every Sunday evening or Monday morning, I take fifteen minutes or so to plan out my week.

Not only does it help me see what I need to accomplish each week, but it also helps me calibrate my weekly tasks within the bigger context of my ultimate vision and purpose. It helps me stay out of the "thick of thin things," as Stephen R. Covey puts it.

3. MONTHLY MASTERMIND SESSIONS

Every purpose-driven person should be part of a mastermind group of carefully-selected people who keep you accountable to your purpose and help you generate ideas and overcome challenges.

Doing this with just one friend recently has been profoundly useful for me. My recommendation is that you keep the group small, three to five people at most.

4. QUARTERLY RETREATS

At least quarterly, step away from your normal routines and take a full day or two to relax, reflect, and brainstorm. Leave all your electronic devices at home. Take a notebook. Put yourself in a completely different environment, whether it be hiking in the mountains or staying at a spa.

Ask yourself if you're clear on your purpose, and if you're on the right path. Write down ideas for accelerating your progress.

5. CONSTANT THINKING & LEARNING

Never let a day pass without learning something new. Read meaningful, inspiring books. Immerse yourself in education and training to develop expertise in your field. Seek out and engage with mentors. Stay curious. Take time to really ponder important thoughts.

The more you think and learn, the greater clarity you gain on your purpose and the more empowered you become to accomplish it.

Without conscious, consistent effort, we drift on the waves of social pressure and casual habits and drown in purposeless routines. The only way to achieve our purpose is to constantly recalibrate our thoughts and actions to our vision and objectives.

THE TWO GREATEST CLUES WHICH REVEAL YOUR UNIQUE MISSION

"Your mission in life," taught the Buddha, "is to find your mission in life and then to give your whole heart and soul to it."

You were beamed to earth, "trailing clouds of glory," for a purpose. You have something noble and profound to accomplish. None other can take your place.

"Let your light shine," commanded Jesus. Your unfulfilled mission is a gaping black hole of squandered potential. Statues will be erected to honor your name when you fulfill your mission.

The challenge is that *finding* mission in the first place is usually tougher than actually living mission.

How many times have you asked God in desperation what to do, while telling Him you'll do whatever He asks if He just shows you the way? I can't speak for you, but for me His answer is almost always, "You think I'd make it that easy for you?" spoken with a sly grin and a hearty chuckle.

Thanks to His calculated evasiveness, I've had to uncover my own clues revealing my mission. I'm certain that the two greatest clues I've unearthed are universal. You can know with conviction that you've been shown the path to mission by:

1. What upsets and angers you about society.
2. What you fear the most.

Fix What Angers You

Reading the backs of cereal boxes chaps my hide. The bland and insipid clichés make me want to strangle each and every obtuse member of the bureaucratic corporate committee who had a hand in castrating the message.

You undoubtedly find it silly that I would even mention something so trivial. But I'm a writer. I notice things like that. In fact, I can't *not* notice them. It's tattooed into my DNA. It's my mission to convey meaning, pierce minds, transform hearts.

You can't help but notice and be angered by certain things, too. Things that other people are clueless about. Things far more important than cereal box ads. **Go fix them; it's your mission to do so. Leap from the couch. Yank the TV cord from the wall. Flee from Facebook. Go. Fix. Them.**

As Michael Strong wrote in *Be the Solution: How Entrepreneurs and Conscious Capitalists Can Solve All the World's Problems*, "...we welcome dissatisfaction as the source of craving for the good. But we never accept whining or criticizing of others or critiques of society.

"If you don't like it, go fix it, go create a world, a community, a subculture in which your ideals can be instantiated, realized, in which you can show us what your vision of beauty and nobility looks like.

"Create a new social reality, so that I can see your dreams come true. I want to see a world in which billions of dreams are coming true constantly.

"Criticize by creating."

Trust & Follow Your Fear

In *The War of Art: Break Through the Blocks and Win Your Inner Creative Battles*, Steven Pressfield writes, "Are you paralyzed by fear? That's a good sign. Fear is good. Like self-doubt, fear is an indicator.

"Fear tells us what we have to do...The more scared we are of a work or calling, the more sure we can be that we have to do it.

"Resistance is experienced as fear; the degree of fear equates to the strength of the Resistance. Therefore the more fear we feel about a specific enterprise, the more certain we can be that that enterprise is important to us and to the growth of our soul.

"That's why we feel so much Resistance. If it meant nothing to us, there'd be no Resistance."

Seth Godin concurs, "If you're afraid of something, of putting yourself out there, of creating a kind of connection or a promise, that's a clue that you're on the right track. Go, do that."

I was scared poopless of the idea of Life Manifestos (LifeManifestos.com). Afraid of flushing time, money, and effort down the drain. Worried sick about launching an uncertain venture then screaming to the earth in a fiery ball of failure. Terrified that my precious pearls would be nothing more than scorned fodder for oblivious swine. Intimidated by the awesome challenge of cramming libraries of wisdom into 150-word manifestos.

So I did it. Because I knew that fear was the call of mission.

What are *you* desperately afraid of? I'm not talking about primal fears like snakes and heights. I'm talking about those intuitions screaming from your soul that you've slammed into a box, locked tightly, buried deeply.

I'm talking about every great idea you've ever had that you've talked yourself out of because the prospect of failure paralyzed you. I'm talking about those venomous butterflies swarming in your gut every time you think of doing _____.

Those fears are a laser pinpointing the exact source and nature of your mission. They are not the storm; they are the lighthouse.

Set your course to point straight at them. Man your rudder, adjust your sails. Square your shoulders. Grit your teeth. Strap on a diaper if necessary. Bellow "Banzai!" and kamikaze through them.

You won't die. You'll come alive for the first time. The universe will shift. And you will know what you were born to do.

No more armchair criticizing. No more fearful paralysis. No more fumbling in the dark groping for mission. Follow the clues of what angers you and what scares you. And through darkness and confusion will burst the brilliant light of mission.

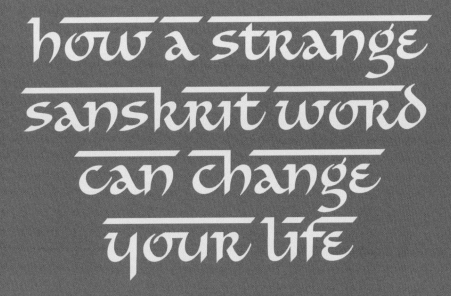

how a strange sanskrit word can change your life

Your path to mission is illuminated by what angers you and what you fear. But there's a deeper principle at the heart of those two clues.

Those two clues shine light on the path. But they are not the path. The path is bliss.

It's ironic, I know. But think it through. Underlying what angers and scares you is what brings you the most rapturous joy.

Anger is a manifestation of passion. Passion is the fuel of purpose. And living on purpose is sheer bliss. Swat your internal butterflies and push through to the other side of fear, and waiting for you is ecstasy, euphoria, exultation.

Follow your anger and fear to discover your path. Then walk the path by following your bliss.

Scholar Joseph Campbell happened upon the power of bliss by studying an ancient Sanskrit word. In *The Power of Myth* he explains, "Now, I came to this idea of bliss because in Sanskrit, which is the great spiritual language of the world, there are three terms that represent the brink, the jumping-off place to the ocean of transcendence: Sat-Chit-Ananda. The word 'Sat' means being. 'Chit' means consciousness. 'Ananda' means bliss or rapture. I thought, 'I don't know whether my consciousness is proper consciousness or not; I don't know whether what I know of my being is my proper being or not; but I do know where my rapture is. So let me hang on to rapture, and that will bring me both my consciousness and my being.'"

hε continues, "I even have a superstition that has grown on me as the result of invisible hands coming all the time–namely, that if you do follow your bliss you put yourself on a kind of track that has been there all the while, waiting for you, and the life that you ought to be living is the one you are living. When you can see that, you begin to meet people who are in the field of your bliss, and they open the doors to you. **I say, follow your bliss and don't be afraid, and doors will open where you didn't know they were going to be.**"

It seems so easy: To find success simply do the things that make you happy.

But why is it so hard, and why do so few people do it? Why are the vast majority of people bored and discontent in jobs they can't stand, leading "lives of quiet desperation," as Thoreau said?

Simple: We're afraid of our bliss. As Marianne Williamson wrote, "Our deepest fear is not that we are inadequate. Our deepest fear is that we are powerful beyond measure. It is our light, not our darkness that most frightens us..." You know the quote.

To appease our conscience—guilty for not following our bliss and living on purpose—we make up stories like: "Following my bliss is self-indulgent and irresponsible. Life isn't a bed of roses, and responsible adults just have to do things they don't like."

On the contrary, following your bliss is the most responsible thing you can do with your life. Ignoring and stifling it is not only irresponsible—it is a direct affront to your Creator, who planted the seeds of your unique bliss in your heart.

There are problems only you can solve, wounds only you can heal. Those problems remain unsolved, the wounds are gaping, the good team is losing while you're jabbering on the sidelines about being a "responsible adult."

You have a sacred duty to God and to humanity to follow your bliss.

And let's be clear: Following your bliss really isn't a bed of roses. As Joseph Campbell clarified, "When I taught in a boys' prep school, I used to talk to the boys who were trying to make up their minds as to what their careers were going to be. A boy would come to me and ask, 'Do you think I can do this? Do you think I can do that? Do you think I can be a writer?'

"'Oh,' I would say, 'I don't know. Can you endure ten years of disappointment with nobody responding to you, or are you thinking that you are going to write a best seller the first crack? If you have the guts to stay with the thing you really want, no matter what happens, well, go ahead.'"

Following your bliss doesn't guarantee instant success. It doesn't mean a pain-free, challenge-less life. It simply guarantees bliss through the process, which means you'll push through the obstacles as long as you stay on the path of bliss.

10 POWER QUESTIONS TO DISCOVER & FOLLOW YOUR BLISS

The following ten questions come from Brian Johnson's book *A Philosopher's Notes: On Optimal Living, Creating an Authentically Awesome Life, and Other Such Goodness.* Write your answers in detail. Your bliss awaits:

1. How can you use your strengths in greatest service to yourself, your family, your community, and the world?

2. How can you get paid to do what you love?

3. What five things are you most proud of? What five things will you be most proud of?

4. If you had all the time and all the money in the world, what would you do?

5. What's your ideal day look like? When do you get up? What do you do? With whom? For whom? Imagine it in vivid detail!

6. Who are your heroes? Why? How are you like them?

7. What would you do if you weren't afraid?

8. If you were guaranteed to succeed, what's the #1 thing you would do?

9. What is it that you and only you can do for the world?

10. How can you live in more integrity with your ideals? What's the #1 thing you could start doing that would have the most positive impact in your life? What's the #1 thing you could stop doing that would have the most positive impact in your life?

Why Passionate People Suffer

The word "passion" has been hijacked. Misused and abused. Emasculated by a feel-good culture of moral relativism. Prostituted by personal development gurus.

Passion today is understood as what excites you. What puts the sparkle in your eyes, the twinkle in your toes. Internet definitions include:

- Strong and barely controllable emotion
- A state or outburst of such emotion
- Intense sexual love
- An intense desire or enthusiasm for something
- A thing arousing enthusiasm

The word has become candy for frivolous children when, at its roots, it is meat for dedicated adults.

Coined by 12th century religious scholars, "passion" means to suffer. In fact, the word was created to describe the "willing suffering of Christ."

In his excellent book, *Aspire: Discovering Your Purpose Through the Power of Words*, Kevin Hall describes a meeting he had with Arthur, a retired 40-year Stanford linguistics professor, who taught him the meaning of passion. Kevin writes,

> *"After educating me about the word's etymology, Arthur added, 'Passion doesn't mean just suffering for suffering's sake; it must be pure and willing suffering.*
>
> *"Arthur said that both 'passion' and 'path' have similar roots: the word 'path' is a suffix that means suffering from.*
>
> *"'Think about it, Kevin,' said Arthur, 'We have doctors called pathologists. They study the illnesses and diseases that humans suffer.'*
>
> *"Then he revealed a link between suffering, or passion, and sacrifice. 'The word sacrifice comes from the Latin sacra, which means sacred, and fice, which means to perform. To sacrifice is to perform the sacred.'*
>
> *"'At its essence,' he continued, 'passion is sacred suffering.'"*

Kevin concludes that, "It's one thing to suffer and be a victim; it's an entirely different thing to be willing to suffer for a cause and become a victor. Even though it has become popular to define passion as deep or romantic love, the real meaning is being willing to suffer for what you love. When we discover what we are willing to pay a price for, we discover our life's mission and purpose."

If passion is simply what makes you happy, you'll quit doing it when it gets tough, when it becomes too risky, when you're ignored and mocked.

Your true passion is what you're willing to do if it kills you.
What you stick with even when it's excruciating. When it's risky.

The things you do because you know they're right. Because you know they'll make a profound difference. The things that simmer in the deepest parts of your soul—far beyond what's fun or what feels good.

As Thomas Paine wrote, "I love the man that can smile in trouble, that can gather strength from distress, and grow brave by reflection. 'Tis the business of little minds to shrink; but he whose heart is firm, and whose conscience approves his conduct, will pursue his principles unto death."

Christ's passion wasn't the superficial bliss of what made him feel good in the moment. It was the cross-carrying, torture-enduring suffering of a Man who understood how and why to sacrifice immediate pleasure for long-term joy.

How about your passion? When asked what you're passionate about, don't tell me what makes you feel good or what excites you. Tell me what you're willing to suffer for.

$27 THAT FOREVER CHANGED THE WORLD

IN early 1970, a man named Muhammad was a Bangladeshi economist at Chittagong University. After a devastating cyclone, bloody war of independence with Pakistan, and severe famine, Bangladesh was suffering deeply. Muhammad was heartbroken over the poverty he saw, knowing his academic economics were doing nothing to alleviate it.

In 1974 he visited a village to learn directly from the people how to help. He discovered that women creating handcrafts were paying local moneylenders interest rates as high as 10 percent per week. He began loaning these women money from his own pocket, starting with just $27.

$27

From that initial $27 investment, Nobel Prize winner Muhammad Yunus built Grameen Bank, which today has 2,565 branches with 22,124 staff serving 8.35 million borrowers (96% women) in 81,379 villages. The microcredit pioneer lends out more than a billion dollars a year in loans averaging less than $200. The bank has lifted millions of illiterate peasants out of the depths of poverty by helping them create small but thriving businesses.

The world is fundamentally, dramatically, and forever changed because one man acted on a prompting to lend twenty-seven bucks to impoverished women making handcrafts.

How many times have you received promptings to help others, start a business, make a difference—and not acted on those promptings? What could those ideas have become? Who could they have helped, no matter how insignificant your actions may have seemed in the moment?

THE GREATEST OPPORTUNITIES DON'T APPEAR AS LUCRATIVE CONTRACTS ON YOUR DESK, BUT AS SUBTLE FLASHES OF INSIGHT IN YOUR MIND.

But they can't unfold if you don't act on them. As Roy H. Williams wrote, "Every door of opportunity begins as a window in your mind. Look through that window of imagination and glimpse a world that could be, someday. Keep looking... Be patient... And watch it grow into a door of Opportunity through which you might pass into an entirely different future. Opportunity never knocks. But it hangs thick in the air all around you. You breathe it unthinking, and dissipate it with your sighs."

This week—like every week of your life—you're going to have at least one idea of how you can create greater value in the world. An idea for a business. A book. An invention. A service project. A thought that you should call a friend. A prompting to read to a child. A feeling to break your routine. A pressing reminder of an idea you've already had.

Your challenge is simple: Write it down immediately, then do something about it. Take one action and see what unfolds.

Or don't act on it. And continue on like nothing ever happened. And indeed, nothing new, surprising, different, or better will ever happen in your life without action.

Your marvelous door of opportunity awaits the simple key of action. Will you turn it?

WHY
GREAT IDEAS
ARE WORTHLESS

"You're just one idea away from a major breakthrough," I once heard a seminar speaker declare, referring to business success.

If only it were that easy. If it were, I'd have "major breakthroughs" every day.

The only ideas that have led to "major breakthroughs" in my life are the ones I've actually acted on.

I was reminded of something else I heard at another seminar: "Don't tell me about your potential. Every bozo living in the street has potential."

Ideas are like potential-worthless without action. Ideas are a dime a dozen. Execution is worth its weight in gold. Execution gives ideas value.

Victor Hugo famously said, "All the forces in the world are not so powerful as an idea whose time has come." Hogwash. All the ideas in the world have no power except those acted on.

"All men are created equal" was nothing but an idea until Revolutionaries suffered, bled, and died for it. "I have a dream" was just that—a dream until civil rights activists acted boldly to achieve that dream and were beat, imprisoned, assassinated. Without the light bulb, Edison is just an unknown crank with a great idea. Without Henry Ford acting on his idea for the auto assembly line, his company wouldn't exist.

Alone, an idea is a seed without soil and water. Christ taught how to manifest true value from ideas in his "Parable of the Sower":

Behold, a sower went forth to sow;

And when he sowed, some seeds fell by the way side, and the fowls came and devoured them up:

Some fell upon stony places, where they had not much earth: and forthwith they sprung up, because they had no deepness of earth:

And when the sun was up, they were scorched; and because they had no root, they withered away.

And some fell among thorns; and the thorns sprung up, and choked them:

But other fell into good ground, and brought forth fruit, some an hundredfold, some sixtyfold, some thirtyfold.

Ideas, like seeds, need spiritually-receptive, hard-working gardeners to make them grow.

If you're not in tune with your intuition, your ideas fall by the wayside. If you flit from project to project with no follow-through, your ideas fall upon stony ground and wither in the sun. The thorns of fear and pessimism, if heeded, will choke your ideas.

Yes, dynamic, creative, innovative thinking is absolutely essential to success. But action is the pilot, ideas are the co-pilot.

Don't wait for an earth-shattering idea before acting. Engage. Move. Do what you can with what you have to the best of your ability.

The more you focus and the harder you work to achieve a goal, the more creative you will become. In fact, your best ideas will come as a result of persistent execution over time. Lights turn on after the wire is laid. As Colleen Barrett said, "When it comes to getting things done, we need fewer architects and more bricklayers."

**People who consistently act on small ideas achieve
more than those with big ideas and no follow-through.
Action yields far more fruit than brainstorming.**

The seeds of ideas can only sprout through action, take root through execution. You can have the greatest ideas in the world and never progress. In truth, you're just an *action* away from a major breakthrough.

HOW TO OVERCOME
INGRATITUDE & DISCOURAGEMENT

Thomas
was born in Bristol, Pennsylvania thirty-six years after the Constitution was ratified.

When Thomas was seven years old, his father was impoverished because of sickness. They were forced to move, and his father put him and his siblings to work in a cotton mill.

Thomas worked in mills and as a calico printer until 1845 when, at the age of twenty, he quit work and left home to, as he put it, "shift for myself." He worked a series of odd jobs, earning five dollars per week at the most. Some of the companies he worked for went out of business, and at times he was unable to collect wages. He finally found dependable work spinning cotton in Gloucester City, New Jersey, where he worked until March of 1847.

At the age of twenty-two, he traveled to St. Louis, joined up with pioneer companies, and headed west. After a three-month journey by wagon, he arrived in Salt Lake City on September 25, 1847.

That winter he had little to eat but "rennet put into milk, which made curd, with a little cream on it, and also thistle tips for greens." But he felt grateful for that, as many of the city's inhabitants were forced to eat rawhide to stay alive.

The next spring, after securing five acres of land, he commenced plowing and planting. Crickets devastated his crops that first year.

The next year he planted twenty-five acres, which again yielded little due to crickets and drought.

But that summer's hardships were alleviated when he met miss Mary Ann, a pretty, curly-haired brunette, whom he married that year at the age of twenty-four.

1850 was a good year for Thomas and Mary Ann. In the spring, they moved into their own cabin on forty acres, enjoyed a good crop yield, and secured a few good animals. To top it off, Mary Ann gave birth to a "fine daughter," also named Mary Ann, on December 14th.

But their good fortune was short-lived. Thomas wrote in his journal, "During the winter, one of the horses died, and about the first of March my cow and calf also died. A large sow pig got poisoned and it died. I had three cats and they died. My dog—someone killed. This was about the amount of my livestock. I now had one horse left with which to continue farming..."

He put his head down and kept working, and they harvested enough that summer to keep going.

After a lifetime of persistent struggle, the man who had been doing a man's work since the age of seven, wrote in his journal "a few words of encouragement to [his] children":

"...you will see that in all of my ups and downs in the world that I had the spirit of perseverance. In my travels through life, when misfortune seemed to press down hard upon me, I always pressed forward the harder and would accomplish that which I undertook to do.

"And when famine and starvation stared me in the face, and hunger had so weakened my mortal frame, that when at labor I would have to sit down to rest in order to gain strength that I might perform my day's work, still I hung on to my faith and integrity in the Lord...

"Therefore, my dear children, let nothing of an evil nature persuade you from a righteous course through life, and carry out your righteous decrees and be firm in your determinations."

And so it is that any time I feel discouraged or ungrateful, I remember Thomas Sirls Terry, my fourth great-grandfather.

What the Chinese Get that Americans Have Forgotten

*A*n ancient Chinese parable is told of Yu Gong, a 90-year-old man whose travels to and from his home were inconvenienced by two large nearby mountains. One day Yu Gong said to his family, "These mountains are too inconvenient. Why not get rid of them?" His son and grandson responded, "What you say is true. We shall start moving them tomorrow." The next day, they began moving the mountain, carrying stones into the sea. They worked nonstop through summer and winter, rain and snow. Observing their work, a man said, "Yu Gong, you are so old. Do you really think it is possible to move the mountains?" Yu Gong responded, "When me and my sons die, my grandchildren will continue, and so on through generation after generation. We will move the stones every day and we will move these mountains."

IN *The Silent Language*, Edward Hall writes, "The future to us is the foreseeable future, not the future of the Asian that may involve centuries...Anyone who has worked in industry or in the government of the United States has heard the following: 'Gentlemen, this is for the long term! Five or ten years.' ...The Asian, however, feels that it is perfectly realistic to think of a long time in terms of thousands of years or even an endless period..."

Consider that China's personal savings rate is 38 percent—compared to America's 3.9 percent.

Generational thinking is a foreign concept to a quick-fix, instant-gratification society fat on fast food, corroded by credit, drowning in the pervasive message that you can have it all and you can have it now.

Our national prosperity has come with consequences. Americans today have confused comfort and convenience with true wealth and lasting impact. Our time horizon has been reduced to looking forward to paychecks, weekends, and vacations. We have largely forgotten how—and why—to leave a legacy. Instead, we leave liabilities.

As Wall Street Journal columnist Peggy Noonan wrote, "People are freshly aware and concerned about the real-world implications of a $1.6 trillion dollar deficit, of a $14 trillion debt. It will rob America of its economic power, and eventually even of its ability to defend itself... And there are the moral implications of the debt...: The old vote themselves benefits that their children will have to pay for. What kind of a people do that?"

The kind of people, Peggy, who value their privileges above their principles, to paraphrase Dwight D. Eisenhower. And because we ignore our principles, we are rapidly losing our privileges, just as Eisenhower warned.

The majority of Americans must learn what the Chinese know, as well as what the minority of wealthy Americans know. The 1970 book *The Unheavenly City* by Harvard University sociologist Edward Banfield details the results of one of the most profound studies on success ever conducted. Banfield set out to discover why certain people become financially independent and others do not. His assumption was that the answer would be found in factors such as family background, education, intelligence, influential contacts, or other similar factors.

He discovered instead a particular mindset shared by the wealthiest, most successful individuals. He called this mindset a "long time perspective." The most successful individuals, he found, considered the future with every decision. The study showed that the longer the time horizon a person considered while planning and acting, the more likely he or she would be to succeed, financially and otherwise.

As Roy H. Williams wrote, "Wealthy people routinely plant seeds that won't bear fruit for months or even years."

What seeds are you planting today that you intend to be harvested by future generations? Are you planting legacy seeds, or liability seeds? Are you moving mountains for future generations, or juggling credit cards for personal pleasure? Is your vision expansive enough to include future generations?

"If your life's work can be accomplished in your lifetime," said Wes Jackson, "you're not thinking big enough."

Why Americans Should Get SMACKED!

Elena Bonner would have smacked Jane Boucher upside her head. And she'd undoubtedly give Americans an earful for our relatively petty complaints.

Forbes reported that "Some surveys have found that 87 percent of Americans don't like their jobs."

Author Jane Boucher commented on the situation, "Most of us can't just quit our jobs."

SMACK!

"Don't whine to me about what you can and can't do in America," I imagine Elena Bonner saying in disgust.

Elena was a Soviet dissident and human rights activist who died in 2011. Knowing her awe-inspiring story, I imagine what she'd say to any American who feels "trapped" for any reason:

"In December of 1985 I was under house arrest in the USSR with my husband, physicist and activist Andrei Sakharov.

"Andrei and I had subjected ourselves to long and terrible hunger strikes to protest the Soviet regime. My physical health had deteriorated so badly that I desperately needed medical attention.

"Gorbachev allowed me to travel to the United States, where I spent six months getting surgery, writing a memoir, and spending time with my family members who had emigrated.

74

"After recovering, there I was, free and comfortable, with a choice to make: to stay in America or to return to my hideous oppression in the Soviet Union.

"Understand that the Communist Party under Stalin had murdered my father and uncle. They had enslaved my mother for eight years in a forced labor camp, and had exiled her for nine more years after that. They had also exiled my aunt.

"In addition to our several hunger strikes, Andrei and I had endured years of exile under the constant watch of the KGB. We had no access to a phone. We were never allowed to leave our tiny, dingy apartment unaccompanied by guards.

"We were accused of numerous crimes against the state. We were constantly accosted, intimidated, and harassed by authorities.

"I could have stayed in America as a defector—free forever from the Soviet nightmare, happy with my family, well-fed and comfortable, immersed in opportunity.

"But under those circumstances, knowing full well what I was going back to, I chose to return to my husband and to continue our struggle together.

"So you can understand why it's ridiculous and offensive to me when free Americans complain about having no opportunity or choice.

"We always have a choice. Yes, there are risks and consequences attached to every choice— believe me, I know that more than anyone.

"But to even imply that one has no choice is an absurd, outrageous, and revolting self-imposed limitation. It is to spit in the face of anyone who has suffered under oppressive regimes; to ignore the blood spilled and awful sacrifices made by those who secured your freedom. It is to be imprisoned behind bars of your own making.

"In America you can choose to do what you love. Or you can choose to love what you do. But never can you say—without gross self-deception—that you just don't have a choice in the matter.

"You are not a helpless child waiting for a master to tell you what to do. You are not trapped in your job.

"If you don't like something, you can change it. If you see something that needs improving, you can fix it. If you want a better life, you can fight for it. If you want more money, you can produce and earn more.

"So stop whining about being trapped. Choose what you want to do and become. And don't make me smack you upside your head."

Why Comfort is a Curse

WE BURST FROM THE WOMB, WIDE-EYED, HUNGRY FOR DISCOVERY, THIRSTY FOR ADVENTURE. EYES PROBING, FINGERS POKING, TONGUES LICKING, MINDS CHEWING, BUBBLING THROUGH LIFE IN CONSTANT, EXULTANT MOTION. JOYFULLY DISTURBED ARE WE, JITTERING WITH AN INSATIABLE "WHY," RAPTUROUS WITH POSSIBILITY, TAKING NOTHING FOR GRANTED.

BUT OVER TIME, OUR FLAMES OF CURIOSITY ARE EXTINGUISHED. WE SUCCUMB TO ADULTHOOD, OUR ZEST FOR LIFE DROWNED BY ROUTINE AND RESPONSIBILITY, OUR INNOCENT CURIOSITY SUFFOCATED AND REPLACED BY VAIN AMBITION, THE THRILL OF DISCOVERY STRANGLED BY APATHETIC COMFORT.

Renowned psychologist Mihaly Csikszentmihalyi reveals how creative people are cultivated and how they keep the spark alive in his enlightening book *Creativity: Flow and the Psychology of Discovery and Invention*. He writes, "Without a burning curiosity, a lively interest, we are unlikely to persevere long enough to make a significant new contribution...Someone who is motivated by the desire to become rich and famous might struggle hard to get ahead but will rarely have enough inducement to work beyond what is necessary, to venture beyond what is already known."

Misguided ambition is but a confectionary counterfeit of meat-and-potatoes curiosity. It may provide an initial spark of energy, but it quickly burns out and fades. Even when we achieve such ambitions, we're left empty and unfulfilled.

CHILDLIKE CURIOSITY IS THE EVERLASTING FUEL OF JOYFUL, CREATIVE LIVING.

Seek not, therefore, to make a name for external validation, but to make new discoveries for the intrinsic thrill.

One element of Csikszentmihalyi's research lunged from the page and held me riveted: "Many creative individuals came from quite poor origins and many from professional or upper-class ones; very few hailed from the great middle class.

"About 30 percent of the parents were farmers, poor immigrants, or blue-collar workers However, they didn't identify with their lower-class positions and had high aspirations for their children's academic advancement...

"Only about 10 percent of the families were middle-class. A majority of about 34 percent had fathers who held an intellectual occupation, such as professor, writer, orchestra conductor, or research scientist. The remaining quarter were lawyers, physicians, or wealthy businessmen...

"Clearly it helps to be born in a family where intellectual behavior is practiced, or in a family that values education as an avenue of mobility—but not in a family that is comfortably middle-class."

Ah. Perpetually creative people are disturbed and curious — either made so by circumstance or natural appetite.

COMFORT KILLS MORE DREAMS THAN FAILURE.

Furthermore, "Curiosity will conquer fear even more than bravery will," as James Stephens said. Is it any wonder, then, that the Man who promised life eternal and abundant exhorted us to become as little children?

The most critical quest of adulthood is to stay joyfully disturbed and innocently engaged by insatiable curiosity. To those wallowing in middle-class comfort, lounging in middle-class sofas, watching middle-class sitcoms, I say drop to your knees and plead in the words of Sir Francis Drake:

Disturb us, Lord, when we are too well pleased with ourselves,
When our dreams have come true because we have dreamed too little,
When we arrived safely because we sailed too close to the shore.

Disturb us, Lord, when with the abundance of things we possess
We have lost our thirst for the waters of life...

Disturb us, Lord, to dare more boldly, to venture on wider seas
Where storms will show your mastery;
Where losing sight of land, we shall find the stars.

We ask You to push back the horizons of our hopes;
And to push into the future in strength, courage, hope, and love.

To contradict Marx, undisturbed comfort is the opiate of the masses. And for numbed, adult souls, the best rehab is childlike curiosity.

Livin' the Dream, Baby

Sometimes life just sucks and there's no way around it.

My family was on a trip when, an hour and a half into our drive, five-year-old Avery started moaning about an upset stomach. The moans escalated into wails, then became incessant, intolerable shrieks.

Thirteen-year-old Alex and seven-year-old Libby begged her to stop, which did nothing but add to the noise. Queen Karina anxiously searched for the next exit while I took Avery into my lap to try to calm her down. Jealous that Avery got to be unbuckled, three-year-old Laela got into the act, howling that she wanted me to hold her too.

We found an exit, pulled off into a Subway parking lot, and dragged the whole caravan inside with no shortage of weeping, wailing, and gnashing of teeth. Everyone went to the bathroom—a tedious process, as anyone with kids can attest.

Then Laela started acting up, so Karina took her outside for a time out. Meanwhile, Avery said she was cold, so I went back to the car to get her jacket.

As I passed Karina dealing with stubborn Laela, I gave her a kiss and said, "We're livin' the dream, baby, livin' the dream."

Yeah, it was sarcastic. But it's also true.

Not for anything would I trade my family pandemonium, complete with ear-piercing shrieking, poopy diapers, discarded suckers clinging to the carpet, food spills, stepping on sharp toys in the middle of the night, and sleep deprivation.

REAL-LIFE DREAMS AREN'T DEVOID OF CHALLENGES; THEY'RE DEFINED AND ENHANCED BY THEM.

As Gordon B. Hinckley said, "Anyone who imagines that bliss is normal is going to waste a lot of time running around shouting that he's been robbed. The fact is that most putts don't drop, most beef is tough, most children grow up to just be people, most successful marriages require a high degree of mutual toleration, most jobs are more often dull than otherwise. Life is like an old time rail journey: delays, sidetracks, smoke, dust, cinders and jolts, interspersed only occasionally by beautiful vistas and thrilling burst of speed. The trick is to thank the Lord for letting you have the ride."

Sometimes all we can do is hang on and endure. We may not be floating on clouds of bliss, but we don't have to be miserable, either.

Conscious gratitude goes a long way in these situations. We can widen our lens and see a bigger picture. While Avery was shrieking, we were driving in a perfect car on perfect roads in a free country with money in the bank. We have family and friends who love us. We have perfect health. I'm able to earn a great living doing what I love from the comfort of my home. We have cell phones that connect with people across the country, take pictures and record videos, check email, give us driving directions. A thousand more amazing blessings could easily be counted.

It's also helpful to remember that each stage in life comes with its own set of challenges, along with its own blessings. Our little three-year-old Laela Grace unrolls the toilet paper and leaves ice on the floor from the refrigerator ice dispenser now. But she also says "You my bes' frien' ever be" so sweetly it makes my heart ache. When she grows out of the menacing phase, we'll also lose so much of what we love about her. She wakes us up almost every night now. But we know there will come a day when we'll long for the middle-of-the-night cuddling we get with her as a result.

Every time our little kids wreak havoc and we feel like we've reached our limits, Queen Karina and I look at each other and start singing the song "You're Gonna Miss This"
by Trace Adkins:

> You're gonna miss this,
> You're gonna want this back
> You're gonna wish these days
> Hadn't gone by so fast.
> These are some good times,
> So take a good look around
> You may not know it now
> But you're gonna miss this.

So when life sucks, just hang on and remember it will get better. It's rarely as bad as it seems in the moment. And it's all part of livin' the dream.

The Only Sure Path to True Greatness

"To every man there comes," said Winston Churchill, "...that special moment when he is figuratively tapped on the shoulder and offered the chance to do a special thing unique to him and fitted to his talent. What a tragedy if that moment finds him unprepared or unqualified for the work which would be his finest hour."

You were born for greatness. But how do you prepare for it? Through years of tireless, thankless, recognition-less goodness.

Mother Teresa was an unknown nun in India who humbly served the poor, sick, orphaned, and dying for twenty-nine years before her goodness was recognized with a Nobel Price in 1979.

George Washington transcribed his "Rules of Civility & Decent Behavior" as a teenager and strove to live them for years until he eventually was called to become the revolutionary general and later our nation's first president.

Rosa Parks was little more than a good woman, a domestic worker virtually unknown to the world. Until one day, on an obscure Alabama bus in 1955, she sat down, tired, and felt a soft tap on her shoulder.

True greatness cannot be achieved in the absence of goodness. More precisely, sustained goodness is the only reliable foundation of and certain path to greatness. As Aristotle said, "I count him braver who overcomes his desires than him who conquers his enemies, for the hardest victory is over self."

BE NOT DECEIVED BY PUBLIC ACCLAIM; rarely does it evidence true greatness. Alexander the supposed Great was in fact a ruthless, brutal, murderous tyrant. We call men great who fight and achieve high public office, yet who privately surrender to the lowest temptations.

Greatness is not ambition, notoriety, or charisma, which afford shortcuts to worldly exaltation. True greatness, like sincere goodness, offer no shortcuts and promise no glory. They do, however, guarantee inner peace with the knowledge that, at any given moment, we are in the right place, at the right time, doing the right thing for the right reasons.

Millions of people are starving and suffering across the globe. America is in steep decline and our Constitution is hanging by a thread. Our national debt has reached astronomical proportions.

You may feel a shoulder tap about these or other monumental problems now. But if *not*, what can you do about them today?

You can fill your mind with wholesome, uplifting material and avoid degenerate and frivolous media. You can resist temptation when no one else will ever know. You can eat and live healthy.

> *"Better keep yourself clean and bright; you are the window through which you must see the world."*
>
> -George Bernard Shaw

You can read to and play with your children. You can listen to them intently when they want to share something they're excited about. You can embrace your spouse and say "I love you" frequently and sincerely. You can be faithful to your spouse both in word and deed.

You can change diapers, wash dishes, vacuum floors, and fold clothes day in and day out for years.

You can help your neighbors. You can serve at homeless shelters. You can say "I'm sorry" to those you've wronged. You can forgive, even when it's hard. You can strive to be honest with yourself. You can swallow your pride and control your anger.

You can spend more time reading books than watching TV.

You can be true to your word and do what you say you're going to do. You can tell the truth when you have nothing to gain and everything to lose. You can live worthy to feel the tap when it comes.

And always, as you work in the trenches of goodness, you must keep your eye on the prize of greatness, your compass aligned with mission. As Henry David Thoreau said, "I have learned, that if one advances confidently in the direction of his dreams, and endeavors to live the life he has imagined, he will meet with a success unexpected in common hours."

True greatness is achieved through seemingly small and simple means. If you feel called to greatness, a stirring in your soul, remember this: **Lofty ideals are achieved through day-to-day living on the ground**.

To quote Thoreau again, "If you have built castles in the air, your work need not be lost; that is where they should be. Now put the foundations under them."

Build your greatness on the foundation of goodness. And you will be prepared to seize your finest hour when you feel the divine tap on your qualified shoulder.

Why Being Great is BORING

"How long did it take you to prepare that sermon?" asked someone of the great minister Dr. Lyman Beecher.

His prompt reply: "Forty years."

When asked how long it would take to learn the violin, the virtuoso violinist Felice Giardini replied, "Twelve hours a day for twenty years." And that was coming from a child prodigy on the instrument.

After the great Polish pianist Paderewski played before Queen Victoria, the queen exclaimed, "Mr. Paderewski, you are a genius!"

"Ah, Your Majesty," he said, "perhaps; but before I was a genius I was a drudge."

Masters make their work look deceptively easy. Amateurs gaze up at their pedestals with stars in their eyes, dreaming of fame and fortune, anxiously searching for shortcuts.

Everyone wants the glamour and glory. But incredibly few are willing to do the arduous, prolonged, behind-the-scenes work required for public success. There are no shortcuts to success.

We must dig in boring trenches before we can plant our illustrious flag on the mountain.

When we watch the movie Gandhi, we see a magnificent leader conquering a powerful empire. What we don't see are the lonely years he spent in law school hunched over mind-numbing textbooks in libraries, tediously memorizing case law.

We marvel at Bill Gates' net worth. What we don't see is the years he spent coding seven days a week through all hours of the night in the computer center at the University of Washington.

We groove to the Beatles' rock-star albums. But what we've never heard is the music they played in Hamburg, Germany clubs for eight hours a night, seven days a week for years, nor have we seen their hard-earned calluses.

Ninety-nine percent of dazzling success is solitary, monotonous work. **You'll never receive genius-level inspiration if you're not willing to endure grunt-level perspiration.**

As Steven Pressfield counsels in *Turning Pro*, "We're all nothing without the Muse. But the pro has learned that the goddess prizes labor and dedication beyond any theatrical seeking of her favors. The professional does not wait for inspiration; he acts in anticipation of it. He knows that when the Muse sees his butt in the chair, she will deliver."

Achieving greatness requires more willful stamina than natural talent. Furthermore, the most honorable things in life rarely receive praise. As P.J. O'Rourke wisely observed, "Everybody wants to save the world, but nobody wants to help Mum with the dishes."

Helen Keller added, "I long to do great and noble things. But it is my destiny to do small things in great and noble ways."

Taking out the trash or washing dishes may not make headlines, but the world turns on such seemingly insignificant acts performed by humble servants.

So stop gazing upwards at spotlights on stages. Pick up your shovel, and start digging the ground at your feet. Stop waiting for inspiration and sit your butt in the chair day in and day out. Keep the dream alive in your heart, but put your shoulder to the wheel.

For how long? For as long as it takes to become great.

What UFO Cults & Killers Reveal About Our Moral Blind Spots

How can human beings gleefully slaughter 800,000 of their brothers and sisters in 100 days using nothing but machetes?

The same way we justify poor health habits and irresponsible credit card use, and for the same reasons we scream in rage at referees when they make a call against our team, then cheer raucously when they make a call against the "enemy."

Whether we're talking about genocide, heated political debates, or little white lies, our daily justifications and rationalizations are explained by "cognitive dissonance," a phenomenon labeled in 1956 by social psychologist Leon Festinger.

Wikipedia defines cognitive dissonance as "a discomfort caused by holding conflicting cognitions (e.g., ideas, beliefs, values, emotional reactions) simultaneously. In a state of dissonance, people may feel surprise, dread, guilt, anger, or embarrassment. The theory...proposes that people have a motivational drive to reduce dissonance by altering existing cognitions, adding new ones to create a consistent belief system, or alternatively by reducing the importance of any one of the dissonant elements."

Put simply, it is a psychological mechanism that drives us toward internal consistency between our beliefs and behaviors.

Festinger coined the term after observing the reactions of a UFO cult when their prophecy that the world would end on December 21, 1954 failed to materialize. Rather than conforming their beliefs to reality, they simply changed their beliefs: Their founder proclaimed that they had spread so much light that God had decided to save the world from destruction.

Tribal Hutus during the 1994 Rwandan genocide performed similar mental acrobatics to justify the slaughter of 800,000 defenseless men, women, and children with machetes in a 100-day period. Rakiya Omaar, director of the human rights organization African Rights, explained, "In Rwanda they referred to Tutsis as cockroaches. They were not human beings...[They said,] 'Don't worry, you're not killing humans like you. You are killing some vermin that belongs under your shoe. You're killing cockroaches.'"

The cognitive dissonance aroused by killing another human being is far too vexing for anyone to handle. But no one thinks twice about killing cockroaches. Problem solved.

Yes, I understand that you and I have not engaged in genocide. But our daily justifications are merely a difference in degree, not a difference in kind. The twisted mental process used by the Hutus is the exact same we use to justify overspending, overeating, mistreating others, and other selfish and destructive behaviors.

Ironically, rather than being a mechanism for self-deception, cognitive dissonance could be leveraged as a powerful tool of improvement.

Yet human nature being what it is, we take the path of least resistance. It's easier to assure ourselves, when buying clothes with credit cards, that a pay raise is forthcoming, rather than waiting to pay cash for the clothes. It's easier to believe we can fix our bodies later, rather than to exercise regularly and eat right. It's easier to believe that others were in the wrong in disagreements than it is to see our own faults and to forgive. It's easier for die-hard conservatives to believe that liberals are completely wrong on all points (and vice versa) than it is to study all political perspectives in depth with an open mind and find the truth in all.

COGNITIVE DISSONANCE USUALLY MAKES OUR LIVES SIMPLER, BUT WORSE.

So how can you leverage it to your advantage—to actually become a better person? By aligning beliefs and behaviors with a standard of moral absolutes that transcends both.

Cognitive dissonance is not concerned with what's right, good, or true. It simply seeks consistency between beliefs and behaviors. Thus, cognitive consonance is achieved and discomfort alleviated when the two align—even if either or both of them are morally reprehensible.

Insert a third component of moral absolutes and it changes the whole equation. Now, rather than simply trying to align two limited and incomplete components, the two are guided by a transcendent standard.

And how do we find moral absolutes? My friend Rachel DeMille provides one answer with what she calls her religion: "Absolute adherence to conscience." In other words, we already know what's right and wrong. It's inside us in that still, small voice. We must live to be worthy to hear that voice, and follow it without question or hesitation.

Secondly, we must be lifelong, committed truth-seekers. We must develop an insatiable appetite for learning and personal growth. We must earnestly seek out what Aristotle, Plato, C.S. Lewis, Leo Tolstoy, James Allen, and countless other thinkers reveal about moral absolutes. We must study history to see where Nero and Caligula went wrong, to understand how the Holocaust happened, to grapple with the intense moral dilemmas faced by leaders. This is the essence of liberal arts education, and why it is so vital for every citizen.

Righteousness and cognitive consonance are not the same thing. Mere consistency between beliefs and behaviors is a poor and misguided substitute for legitimate moral rectitude.

UFO cult followers and murderers are crazy. And so are you and I when we fall prey to cognitive dissonance in the absence of moral absolutes.

TWO WORDS TO

The year is 1910. At 808 Brady Street in Davenport, Iowa, we join two of the most brilliant minds of the 20th Century conversing over dinner.

"Tell me, B.J." says Elbert, "What are the two most valuable words in the English language?"

"I haven't given it much thought," B.J. responds. "What are yours?"

Elbert leans forward and confides, "Survival value."

B.J. ponders the words for a moment. "To be frank, Elbert, I don't see much in them."

"Give them time, B.J. They will grow on you."

"Do explain, Elbert. I'm all ears."

Elbert thoughtfully takes a sip of wine, then pushes his chair back from the table. Eyes gleaming, he speaks earnestly and deliberately, in the manner of a man revealing thoughts he has been pondering for years:

"That which lives after the action itself is complete, is survival value. Actions have survival value according to the degree of good that grows out of them.

"For instance, the man who planted the tree had the joy of doing; the tree adds to the value of his real estate; but the tree will exist long after the man has turned to dust.

"All worthy deeds, all honest work, all sincere expressions of truth—whether by pen or voice—have a survival value.

"Civilization is a great, moving mass of survival values, augmented, increased, bettered, refined, by every worthy life. Man dies, but his influence lives and adds to the wealth, the happiness and the welfare of the world.

"Hate, revenge, jealousy, doubt, negation, have no survival value. Courtesy, kindness, goodwill, right intent, all add to the sum of human happiness. Not only do they benefit the individual who gives them out, but they survive in various forms and add to the well-being of the world.

MEASURE YOUR VALUE

"All acts, whether work or play, should be judged with the idea of survival value in mind.

"Health and happiness are the results of a multiplicity of thoughts and actions possessing survival value.

"Hell might be defined as the sum total of acts which possess no survival value."

The words were spoken by Elbert Hubbard, writer, publisher, artist, philosopher, and the author of "A Message to Garcia," which sold more than 40 million copies in his lifetime, outselling every other publication except the Bible and the dictionary.

B.J. Palmer, the pioneer and developer of Chiropractic, later said that these words became a landmark in his thinking. He also added four more words to the equation: Accumulative Constructive Survival Value and Accumulative Destructive Survival Value.

He explains in his book *Evolution or Revolution*, "What a person makes of his time–thinking, saying, and doing–are accumulative, day after day, year after year; and as they accumulate they are either constructive for welfare of man, or destructive, injuring with whom he commingled.

"Elbert Hubbard's life had an Accumulative Constructive Survival Value. Hitler's life was that of Accumulative Destructive Survival Value."

How about *your* life? What is your survival value? Is it accumulatively constructive or destructive? Or does it hover somewhere in the middle because you're too afraid or apathetic to take a stand either way?

If you're not striving for excellence, you're slipping into mediocrity. As Elbert Hubbard declared, "The man who has nothing to offer the world that the world needs, should telephone the undertaker, for he is a dead one, whether he knows it or not."

The greater value you create for others, the wider your influence spreads and the longer it lasts. Elbert Hubbard died in 1915. But his influence is still felt today because of his survival value. What will people write about you a hundred years after you die?

WHY THE FEELING OF SECURITY MAKES US LESS SECURE

Oblivious to the danger behind us, Queen Karina and I drove for several days before the awful realization: Our two-year-old was buckled tightly into her car seat. But her car seat itself had not been buckled with the seatbelt.

We *felt* safe and secure every time we strapped her in. But had we crashed, that feeling of security would have been ejected and overwhelmed by unforgiving realities.

How often in life do we confuse true security with a false sense of security?

In reality, we don't confuse the two; we choose false security because it's easier. Achieving true security requires hard work and brutal self-honesty. In fact, we'll give almost anything to soothe our fears with the feeling of security—even our freedom. And in so doing, we lose the true security that can only come from accepting the responsibility of freedom.

They don't call them "golden handcuffs" for nothing. Like Esau of old, we sell our birthright of greatness for the pottage of "safe" and cubicled mediocrity. Oblivious to danger, we ride through life—until we're stifled by bureaucracy, ignored by management, ejected by a crashed economy, and our feelings of safety and security are exposed as a cruel joke.

Only by embracing freedom—with all its risks—do we find real security. Not the false security imposed by "benevolent" caretakers, but the true security of resolute self-reliance and battle-hardened grit.

Tom Robbins wrote, "Somewhere in the archives of crudest instinct is recorded the truth that it is better to be endangered and free than captive and comfortable."

I wish I could believe in that instinct. History and current society suggest otherwise. As John Adams argued, "The numbers of men in all ages have preferred ease, slumber, and good cheer to liberty, when they have been in competition. We must not then depend alone upon the love of liberty in the soul of man for its preservation."

The ancient Israelites provided a perfect example of this when they whined to Moses,

94

"Would to God we had died by the hand of the Lord in the land of Egypt, when we sat by the flesh pots, and when we did eat bread to the full; for ye have brought us forth into this wilderness, to kill this whole assembly with hunger."

Freedom comes with a price. But so does false, misguided security. Which price are you willing to pay?

Jacob, second son of Isaac, paid the right price and became a father of nations, a prosperous prince of God. Esau? A despised footnote in history.

The ancient Athenians chose wrong, and history records the result. Historian Edward Gibbon writes, "In the end, more than freedom, they wanted security. They wanted a comfortable life, and they lost it all—security, comfort, and freedom. When the Athenians finally wanted not to give to society but for society to give to them, when the freedom they wished for most was freedom from responsibility, then Athens ceased to be free and was never free again."

Benjamin Franklin put it bluntly: "They that can give up essential liberty to obtain a little temporary safety deserve neither liberty nor safety."

What personal Pharaohs hold you captive and extort your birthright? Fear? Pride? Laziness? Social programming? Addiction? Are you comfortable with your Pharaohs, or are you willing to join with Patrick Henry in proclaiming, "Give me liberty, or give me death!"?

Will you sell out to false security and lose both your security and your freedom? Or are you willing to stay hungry and free through the wilderness of life until you reach the promised land?

In the absence of freedom and responsibility, security is nothing but a delusional feeling. No matter how safe you may feel, dangers much more painful and insidious than temporary hunger and economic struggle loom behind you.

"The old man was right. Only the farmers won. We lost. We always lose."

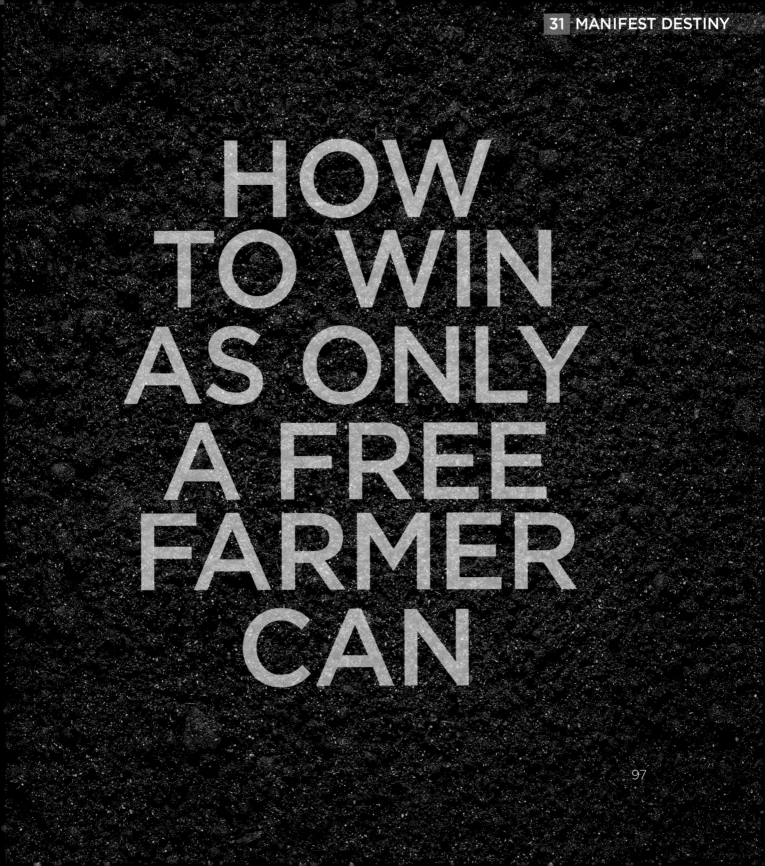

HOW TO WIN AS ONLY A FREE FARMER CAN

"ONLY THE FARMERS HAVE WON," the village elder remarks as he bids farewell to the hired gunmen. "They remain forever. They are like the land itself... You are like the wind—blowing over the land and passing on."

And the three surviving gunmen in the final scene of the western classic The Magnificent Seven ride off into the sunset. They turn to gaze at the village they've just helped to defend—at great personal loss—against marauding bandits.

The final words of the movie, pregnant with metaphoric meaning, are uttered by the main character, hired gun Chris Adams: "The old man was right. Only the farmers won. We lost. We always lose."

Thirty-three years before The Magnificent Seven was released, American architect and social critic Ralph Adams Cram said it more plainly: "Today here in the United States there is a class of men and women, perhaps the majority, that is unfree. I mean all those who subsist on a wage...that is paid to them by those who are, in actuality, their masters; a wage that may be withdrawn at any time and for any reason, leaving them to go on the dole, or to starve, if they can find no new job...These are not free men in any rational and exact sense of the word."

So what constitutes being "free"? Cram answers, "...he only is a free man who owns and administers his own land, craft, trade, art or profession and is able, at necessity, to maintain himself and his family therefrom."

The Distributist League Manifesto, as mentioned in the mind-expanding book *Beyond Capitalism and Socialism*, adds, "The independent farmer is secure. He cannot be sacked. He cannot be evicted. He cannot be bullied by landlord or employer. What he produces is his own: the means of production are his own. Similarly the independent craftsman is secure, and the independent shopkeeper.

"No agreements, no laws, no mechanism of commerce, trade, or State, can give the security which ownership affords. A nation of peasants and craftsmen whose wealth is their tools and skill and materials can laugh at employers, money merchants, and politicians. It is a nation free and fearless. The wage-earner, however sound and skillful his work, is at the mercy of the usurers who own that by which he lives..."

BEYOND ECONOMICS, THERE ARE MUCH DEEPER REASONS WHY OWNERS ALWAYS WIN.

Ownership is far more than having material possessions. It is a mindset, a worldview, a way of life, which can be cultivated whether you're a farmer, an entrepreneur, or an employee.

> **First and foremost, owners own their lives and their choices. They take ultimate responsibility for their results. No whining, no blaming, no justifying or excusing. When staring up from the bottom of the pit of failure, resolute owners declare, "I own this. And I will fix this and succeed if it kills me."**

The owner has something worth fighting and dying for. He is deeply, soulfully married to his work. His purpose is clear, his commitment firm. The fruits of his labors taste sweeter than any wage-earner can imagine. Beware the man who dares deprive him of them.

Time clocks are utterly foreign, incomprehensible devices to the owner. He toils day and night, grinds through holidays, sweats over weekends to manifest his vision as reality. When he's not performing his work, he's dreaming and scheming about it.

The owner is an artist, never content with a final product, ever yearning for perfection.

The owner does not cut corners. He does it right the first time, every time—no matter who else will know. He strives for excellence not to receive praise, but because he couldn't live with himself otherwise.

The owner sacrifices immediate gratification for long-term freedom. He lives in a car and chokes down rice and beans to save money while his friends call him crazy.

The owner thinks generationally. He connects his daily choices with the impact they will have on his children, grandchildren, great-grandchildren and beyond.

Yes, the old man was right: You can be a hired hand who blows through life like the wind, running from your true purpose, never sinking roots. Or you can be an owner whose roots and fruits remain forever...

A Tribute to the American Dream(ers)

The American Dream, though dimmed by bad laws and bad news, is still alive.

I know this because Queen Karina and I discovered Shark Tank, an enthralling TV show for entrepreneurs and investors. After watching the first season, I found myself overwhelmed to the point of tears with a deep respect and even reverence for the American Dream and those who dare dream it.

I honor you, the Dreamers, Risk-Takers, Pioneers, Innovators, Entrepreneurs, and Producers, upon whose intrepid backs has been built the greatest country in the history of the world.

HERE'S TO YOU WHO LIVE THE MEASURE OF YOUR CREATION—TO BE A CREATOR.

Who are driven by a glorious dissatisfaction borne of the fierce belief that anything can be done better. Who are consumed by a holy yet irreverent curiosity. Whose vision of possibility trumps your fear of failure.

You scheme and plan, wonder and brainstorm, tinker and experiment, try and fail, learn and keep moving forward.

You think far beyond a nine-to-five existence. You are motivated by internal passion and purpose rather than 401(k)s and benefits. You seize your own destiny. You are not shielded by committees or corporate coffers. You live and die by your own actions and decisions. Your only safety net is your tenacity and perseverance.

You make no excuses, place no blame, ask no favors. You shoulder responsibility without hesitation. You have crossed your Rubicon resolutely, burned your ships courageously. You have risen from ashes and rubble to triumph against all odds.

Your eyes lift to the heavens to gaze at your North Star, then your hands and back dig trenches on the ground.

Your sleepless nights have led to brighter tomorrows for all of us. Your mortgaged homes and maxed-out credit cards have made us all richer. Your stress and indigestion have made us all happier.

When everyone called you crazy, you listened instead to the most sane voice on earth: your heart. When the facts were stacked against you, you trusted intuition.

Like Don Quixote, you see giants where others only see windmills. You dream the Impossible Dream, reach for the Unreachable Star.

Your back is quivering with thoughtless arrows fired by small-minded detractors. Your heart is heavy with the weight of portentous decisions. But your dream is bright, your resolve unwavering.

Yes, here's to you, American Dreamer, for carrying the divine torch of the American Dream. Here's to anyone who's ever had the guts to join a network marketing company, cold call, or pound the pavement in the audacious pursuit of your dreams.

The politicians and bureaucrats can try to stifle you. They can tax you. They can regulate you. They can sneer down their noses at you and call you greedy and selfish—while living off the fruits of your labors.

But they cannot break your spirit. Nor can they ever beat you. Because their laws and guns are no match for your idea might. Because you will always be one step ahead. Because you understand and live according to natural law. Because you, unlike them, are not blinded by scarcity. Because you know we live in an abundant world, bursting with infinite wealth and opportunity for all. Because you create wealth and opportunity while they suffocate it. Because you truly serve humanity while they smother human potential with excuses and crutches.

So dream on, American Dreamer, and keep the dream alive for us all. We desperately need your heart, your strength, your light. For it is you who will pull our nation from despair and rebuild our City on a Hill.

WHY EVERYONE SHOULD ALWAYS BE IN SALES

I love a man with an agenda.

Almost every time I see my friend John he talks to me about his network marketing company in an attempt to recruit me. He looks me in the eye and speaks with boldness and purpose. He doesn't weasel around the bush. His invitations are clear and direct. I know he cares for me and believes that his product can improve my life.

His solicitations don't bother or offend me in the slightest. I have nothing but respect and admiration for his willingness to overcome his fear and make a better life for himself and his family. I would think less of him if he didn't try to sell me. His commitment is refreshing and infectious.

I wonder why we have such an instinctive aversion to salesmen and network marketers. I wonder why we post "No Soliciting" signs on our houses, then go inside and pump our brains full of TV ads.

Do door-to-door salesmen somehow pose more of a threat to our pocketbook than multi-national corporations with billion-dollar advertising budgets? Why are we okay with McDonald's, Taco Bell, and Frito Lay selling us health-crippling junk but not okay with our friends selling us health supplements? What makes the agendas of corporate advertisers legitimate and network marketers' illegitimate?

Truth is, people with agendas rule the world. And if we don't have a clearly-defined, passionate agenda of our own, we're pawns of those who do.

An agenda is passion, purpose, and commitment. It is knowing who you are, what you stand for, what you believe in. It means having something to offer that improves people's lives. *Everyone* should have an agenda—a clear purpose that the world knows about. Something you're trying to sell—yes, I said SELL—to the world.

> *People with no agenda are to be pitied; they take orders from those who do. As Steve Jobs put it, "If you don't build your dreams, someone else will hire you to build theirs."*

Certainly, we have every reason to be uneasy around weasels with hidden agendas and ulterior motives. Snakes in the grass with unethical agendas should be avoided like the plague. And of course there are always selfish and pushy salesmen who don't respect our time or wishes, who don't sincerely care about us.

But weasels, snakes, and bulls are no reason to avoid and think less of people with sincere and honorable agendas. Neither should our personal agendas be held hostage by fear of how we will be perceived by others.

The people I respect and admire most are those with clear agendas, a sincere concern for improving lives with their agendas, and the courage to promote their agendas with passion.

- Greg Mortenson's agenda is education for young girls in Pakistan (GregMortenson.com).
- Martin Luther King's agenda was equality.
- Mother Teresa's agenda was charity for the poor.

At the root of the fear of being sold is a lack of an agenda. We only fear being sold or taken advantage of when we don't know who we are, what we want, what we stand for.

Clarity surrounding our personal agenda gives us maturity and confidence. We can listen open-mindedly to the agendas of others without fearing we'll be swayed in a direction we'll regret.

Not having a clear agenda also explains the fear of selling. Fear dissolves when we get in tune with our mission, and purify our motives in promoting it.

Know who you are. Know what you were born to promote and accomplish. Believe in yourself and in what you're offering to the world. Sell your agenda boldly and persistently, with pure motive: a genuine love and sincere concern for bettering people's lives.

Everyone should have an agenda. What's *yours*?

THE FASTEST WAY TO GET TO WHERE YOU WANT TO GO IS TO PICK THE BRAIN OF SOMEONE WHO'S ALREADY BEEN THERE.

THAT'S THE SIMPLE WAY TO PUT IT. TRUTH IS, THERE'S MUCH MORE TO THE FORMULA. UNLESS YOU DO IT THE RIGHT WAY, BRAIN-PICKING IS NOTHING BUT OBNOXIOUS FREELOADING, INEXCUSABLE LEECHING, A PARTICULARLY IRRITATING MANIFESTATION OF BAD FORM.

SUCCESSFUL PEOPLE ARE INTENSELY FOCUSED, PRODUCTIVE, AND MISSION-DRIVEN. THEY VALUE TIME FAR MORE THAN UNSUCCESSFUL PEOPLE DO. THE EASIEST WAY TO GET ON THEIR BAD SIDE IS TO WASTE THEIR PRECIOUS TIME.

HERE'S HOW TO SOLICIT ADVICE THE RIGHT WAY:

1. DON'T HESITATE TO ASK

The first mistake people make when seeking advice is simply being afraid to ask. They see potential mentors as unapproachable.

You'd be amazed by how willing successful people are to help you—provided you approach them in the right way. They have invaluable knowledge, experience, and insights, which they love to share. Who doesn't love to talk about their successes?

2. OFFER VALUE IN EXCHANGE FOR THEIR TIME & KNOWLEDGE

Never contact someone for advice and ask them to spend time responding without offering any value in return. Offer to pay them a specific amount of money for a specific amount of time. Offer to take them to lunch. Get creative in identifying your assets and leverage them to create value.

This is less because they expect and want value from you, but more to prove that you're acting in good form. This is not about them; it's about you. Freeloaders are time and energy vampires from whom successful people run very fast, very far.

Successful people earned their knowledge and insights through years of back-breaking, heart-wrenching labor. Don't offend them and cheat yourself by trying to use them to get quick and easy shortcuts.

3. FOLLOW THEIR ADVICE WITHOUT HESITATION OR DEVIATION

DO NOT EVER ASK ADVICE of a trusted mentor unless you're 100 percent willing to do exactly what they advise—even and especially if you disagree.

If you're offended by advice you solicited, that's a sure sign your heart wasn't right when you asked. If you're not willing to hear it and follow it, don't ask for it.

If you're lucky enough to get a mentor to engage with you, don't blow it by ignoring the advice.

Be certain you're asking the right person, one whom you trust will steer you in the right direction—a legitimate mentor. In other words, don't pester your friends with your problems. That's not productive advice-seeking; it's pointless whining.

The plain truth is that most people don't want workable advice from certified mentors who will propel them to the next level. They want commiseration, comfort, understanding, justification for why they're stuck. What many people really want when they solicit advice is not advice at all, but rather validation that they're right.

We say we need help getting outside of our box. But what we really want is for people to crawl into our box, relate to us, and share our pain.

The only people qualified and able to get you out of your box are those who refuse to crawl inside with you. Friends will cozy up with you inside your box. True mentors won't.

And if you disagree with your mentor, follow his instructions anyway. In most cases, you'll learn through execution that he was right, and why. And if he's wrong, you have to earn the right to break the rules by first learning and following the rules. Follow his instructions and learn the lessons first before taking your own path.

4. DISCERN BETWEEN PESSIMISTIC DREAM-KILLERS & REALISTIC MENTORS

Common phenomenon: People will solicit advice. They won't like what they hear because it clashes with their preconceived notions. So they'll justify not following it by labeling it "negative." Anyone who tells them their plan won't work they call a "dream-killer." And so they stay stuck inside their box, smiling with a positive attitude yet suffering from delusional thinking.

To be sure, dream-killers do exist. But unlike mentors, they are people who haven't traveled the path you want to tread. They offer no solutions, but only worn-out cynicism. These are typically people who have failed themselves and try to justify their own failures by giving you every reason why you can't succeed.

(Here's a little secret about dream-killers: they're usually your family and friends who are stuck inside a similar box at the same level as you.)

In almost every case, legitimate mentors will also tell you things you don't want to hear. It will feel like they're insensitive to your pain while they tear your dream apart. But all they're doing is revealing the same pitfalls they fell into along your same path.

Within minutes, the right mentor can analyze your situation and tell you exactly what you're doing wrong and how to fix it. They're not being negative or insensitive; they're being realistic from hard-earned experience.

You can either be hurt or relieved. Your choice. Just know that the sting you feel from their advice is far less than the agony you'll feel if you don't follow it.

So listen: You can either sing Kumbaya with your friends and cry a river inside your box, or you can get the right mentor to demolish your box and propel you to new levels of success.

But when choosing and engaging with your mentor, don't be a brain-picking scavenger. Be a value-creating, eager student with impeccable follow-through.

THREE PROVOCATIVE WORDS THAT REKINDLE THE THRILL OF LIVING

When dull routines have replaced the thrill, the romance, the beauty, the sheer toe-curling joy of living in this fascinating, God-given world, remember three stimulating words:

1. INSPIRATION
2. ENTHUSIASM
3. EPIPHANY

Note carefully what these words have in common:

INSPIRATION

At its roots, "inspiration" means "immediate influence of God." The essential meaning from the Greek is "God-breathed" or "God-blown."

One definition in Webster's 1836 Dictionary reads, "The infusion of ideas into the mind by the Holy Spirit; the conveying into the minds of men, ideas, notices or monitions by extraordinary or supernatural influence; or the communication of the divine will to the understanding by suggestions or impressions on the mind..."

ENTHUSIASM

"Enthusiasm" comes from the Greek *en theos*, meaning "divinely inspired, possessed by a god."

Notre Dame University theology professor Father John O'Brien explains, "...in the early usage of this term among the ancient Greeks, it literally meant 'God within you.' The Divine Being who is the author and the source of all goodness and beauty and truth, honesty and love. God is in the heart of the individual who is possessed by a vision, who burns with ardor, who is determined to make a dream come true. God is there. God is kindling the fire."

EPIPHANY

An "epiphany," is "the sudden intuitive leap of understanding or comprehension of the essence or meaning of something; an illuminating realization or discovery, often resulting in a personal feeling of elation, awe, or wonder."

Essentially, it is a revelation. It is also defined as "a manifestation of a divine being."

How inspired do you feel? How much enthusiasm permeates your life and work? How often do you experience epiphanies? In other words, how are you allowing God to manifest in, motivate, and direct your life?

When life is drudgery and work a bore, remember the immortal words of Christ: "The kingdom of God is within you."

God, who put the colors in the sky, the flavor in peaches, the harmony in music, and the ecstasy in sex, has already given you everything you need to live with rapture, wonder, and bliss. Your task isn't to breath in inspiration, enthusiasm, and epiphanies from Him, but rather to draw them out of yourself.

YOU must inspire yourself from your inner god. YOU must generate your own enthusiasm. YOU must seek and experience your own epiphanies.

Frustrated with people looking for truth outside of themselves, the old Zen monk, Rinzai, sermonized, "If on your way you meet the Buddha, kill him...O disciples of the truth, make an effort to free yourselves from every object...O you, with eyes of moles! I say to you: No Buddha, no teaching, no discipline! What are you ceaselessly looking for in your neighbor's house? Don't you understand that you are putting a head higher than your own? What then is lacking to you in yourselves? That which you have at this moment does not differ from that of which the Buddha is made."

Emerson put it thus: "A man should learn to detect and watch that gleam of light which flashes across his mind from within, more than the lustre of the firmament of bards and sages."

Your God-given spark of life lies waiting for you to breathe on it.

Trust your intuitions, follow your hunches, develop your ideas, act on your promptings without hesitation and the spark will burst into flames of inspiration and enthusiasm. Epiphanies will explode like fireworks.

God has already breathed life into you. Now you must fan the flames.

THE ONLY WAY TO ACCOMPLISH MONUMENTAL TASKS

THERE ARE, TO BE PRECISE, 471 TILES IN MY SHOWER.

Every week, I'm faced with the task of scrubbing the entire shower. Every week, I inevitably feel overwhelmed by how much surface I have to cover with a tiny scrub brush. I usually start with broad, sweeping strokes trying to cover as much area as possible. Until I realize how much I'm missing.

There's only one way I can clean the shower effectively—and get over the mental block of how big the task is: One. Tile. At. A. Time.

Staring at an entire shower wall is daunting and discouraging. But I can easily and happily do one 4" x 4" area. I start in one corner and focus all my energy and attention on one tile. And when that one's done, I do another. And another. And another. Until eventually I realize I've cleaned the entire shower.

I have a thirty-nine-year-old friend who is married, has three children, has a degree in economics, and has been working in the same industry for fourteen years. Trouble is, his heart is pulling him in another direction. He feels called to complete advanced degrees in psychology and become a therapist. But, understandably, he struggles with the decision because it's such a daunting, overwhelming task to think of the whole process of going back to college and completely switching careers at this stage in his life. He feels immobilized and frustrated.

My advice to him is to cultivate an inspiring, empowering vision of what it will feel like to be in his dream career as a therapist. Forget about the arduous journey and just see and feel the end result. Then, drop his gaze from the future and focus all his energy and attention on one step at a time in the present. Take one online class at a time, one day at a time. And another. And another. Until eventually he's walking across the stage to receive his diploma.

In her liberating book, *The Artist's Way*, creativity coach Julia Cameron reveals how to conquer mental blocks, discover your inner artist, and unleash your creative genius. She explains, "Remember that in order to recover as an artist, you must be willing to be a bad artist. Give yourself permission to be a beginner. By being willing to be a bad artist, you have a chance to be an artist, and perhaps, over time, a very good one.

"When I make this point in teaching, I am met by instant, defensive hostility: 'But do you know how old I will be by the time I learn to really play the piano/act/paint/write a decent play?'

"Yes...the same age you will be if you don't."

You know the quote from Lao Tzu: "The journey of a thousand miles begins with one step." Another Chinese proverb makes his statement more accurate and complete: "To get through the hardest journey we need take only one step at a time, but we must keep on stepping."

It's never too late to accomplish great things—the time is going to pass anyway. It's not too hard—if you focus on one step at a time.

What great and noble task do you feel called to accomplish, but you're hesitating to pursue because it feels too daunting? How will you feel when you're standing at the top of your mountain? What is your first baby step? What tiny little task do you need to do right now, today, to move toward your goal?

Go do it. Put the whole journey out of your mind. Focus entirely on: That. One. Step. Then take another step. And another. And another. And one day you'll look up and realize you're on top of the mountain.

WHY THE LAW OF

Attraction

CAN BE DANGEROUS

Speaking of people to avoid like the plague.

At the top of my list are certain "Law of Attraction" gurus who sing the siren song of "You can have everything you want." It's not that I deny the power of the law, mind you. As my readers know, I understand well how our thoughts influence our lives.

What I reject is the naked appeal to self-interest and self-gratification, which deceives in crippling ways. I reject the overwhelming focus on materialism.

These gurus are like Santa Claus filling the heads of children with fanciful dreams: you, you you, toys, toys, toys, fun, fun, fun, a magical orgy of self-indulgence.

You can have a big, fancy house. You can have a brand new, shiny, expensive car that makes heads turn. You can have all the money you want.

And while their disciples are visualizing all the riches they'll enjoy, the luxury they'll bask in, they're usually ignoring the mission they were called to perform.

Our lives are fundamentally transformed when we stop focusing on what we want, and instead ask God what He would have us do with our lives.

There are higher purposes than self-gratification. There is a filter for our desires called mission. What we want and what we *should* want are often two entirely different things, and often completely at odds with each other.

There's nothing intrinsically wrong with big houses and beautiful cars. There *is* something wrong with focusing on them as our primary goals.

- WEALTH IS A BYPRODUCT OF SERVICE.

- THE HIGHEST SERVICE WE CAN PERFORM IS TO FIND AND LIVE OUR MISSION.

- FULFILLING OUR MISSION AT THE HIGHEST LEVEL REQUIRES SUBMISSION TO GOD.

- SUBMIT TO GOD AND FULFILLMENT AND WEALTH, BEYOND ANYTHING WE WOULD HAVE IMAGINED ALONE, ARE OURS TO ENJOY.

As Christ taught, "Therefore take no thought, saying, What shall we eat? Or, What shall we drink? Or Wherewithal shall we be clothed?...But seek ye first the kingdom of God, and his righteousness; and all these things shall be added unto you."

Had George Washington listened to attraction gurus instead of God, he would have settled down on his farm instead of serving as the Revolutionary War General and two terms as our first president. America's story would undoubtedly have been drastically different.

Had Eric Liddell listened to attraction gurus instead of God, he would have run the 100-meter race in the 1924 Paris Olympics and achieved worldly acclaim at the cost of his spiritual integrity.

Had Florence Nightingale listened to attraction gurus instead of God, she would have enjoyed a privileged life in high society, instead of devoting her life to nursing.

I wonder how Ayn Rand, the atheist prophetess of self-interest, would have lived her life differently and what her books would have said had she listened to God instead of her own desires.

We're all self-interested. But a whole new world opens up when we submit our desires to God and let Him guide and refine our desires. And interestingly, by doing so we become so much wealthier and happier than by following our own desires.

Law of Attraction gurus are right: You *can* have anything you want. But do you know what God wants for you?

HOW TO GET INSPIRED

"So here's my question," she said, searching my face earnestly as if expecting my answer to be a life-changing breakthrough that would solve all her problems.

"How do you get inspired?"

STUNNED AND DUMBFOUNDED, I STARED AT HER FOR A LONG MOMENT.

I had just finished presenting at a Leadership Education conference (TJEd.org). I had stressed the principle "Inspire, Not Require," meaning that quality mentors inspire their students to greatness, rather than requiring them to jump through hoops.

I taught that parents and mentors who struggle with this principle aren't inspired themselves — to be inspiring, one has to be inspired.

She waited expectantly.

As I pondered how to answer such a bewildering question, I looked down at the tile floor—just common gray ceramic tiles you walk on every day without ever thinking of them.

I wondered how the flooring was installed. How long did it take them? What tools did they use? Who invented those tools, and how and when? I wondered how tiles are made. Who discovered the process, and when and how? How has it been improved over time? Why does baking clay make it hard? Where did the clay come from? Where were the tiles produced? Who founded the company that produced them, and why?

I wondered about the workers who installed it. What are their stories? Why did they start installing tile? Do they enjoy it? What are they working for? What do they look forward to? What are their dreams? What television shows do they watch? What books do they read?

Who chose this particular tile color? How did they coordinate when the floor would be tiled in conjunction with every other aspect of constructing the building?

Speaking of color, what makes color? What is color? How do we perceive it? Why do we like some colors and dislike others? Why are there so few pink or purple houses? What materials are used to color tiles? How does that material stay baked into the tiles without rubbing off?

I thought of the water used to make the tiles and mix the grout. What is water? Does "one oxygen atom plus two hydrogen atoms" really explain its essence and explain the miracle of water? How can the same chemical compound take the forms of water, ice, and steam?

What laws and principles of math and science were used to create and install the tiles—principles that the workers and I are completely ignorant of, but if understood, could be leveraged to create value and profit?

How many feet have walked across this tile floor? What brought people here? What were they hoping to learn by coming here? What microbes live on the tile? What do they eat? How do they grow?

I gazed in fascination down at a gray tile floor in a conference center in Round Rock, Texas. In awe, I wondered how many millions of people and what natural resources and machines across the globe combined to produce this one floor.

Mesmerized, I thought reverently: The entire world, all man's accumulated knowledge through centuries, all the hopes and dreams and struggles of humanity, the laws that govern the rotation of planets and the life cycle of stars are at my feet. Studying this tile floor would take me a lifetime, and I would never scratch the surface of everything I could learn by starting right here with this floor.

I felt the urge to remove my shoes; I was standing on holy ground.

And I looked up at her and said, "How is it even possible for anyone to *not* be inspired?"

What's in Your "Inspiration Library"?

It's easy to feel inspired, positive, strong, and optimistic when life is great. When the sun of opportunity is radiating and everything turns out just right.

*B*ut what about those times when we're exhausted from long hours and lack of sleep, bored stiff from stale routines, terrified to take action, tempted by vice, or drowning in depression? What do we do when everything goes wrong and life is dark and uncertain?

That's when we need an "Inspiration Library"—music, videos, movies, and books that are guaranteed, no matter what we're dealing with, to dissolve darkness, make our heart leap from our chest, compel us to dance and sing and sigh with contentment, "You know, it's not that bad. I can make it through this."

Powerful media that lifts our eyes from the ground to refocus on our dreams. That sucks us out of our puddle of self-pity. A slap in the face of negativity that awakens us to see positivity. Light-filled media that snaps us out of the dark reverie of temptation until we declare, "This is not who I am," do an about-face, and valiantly stride away.

Here's your challenge: Gather every video, song, movie, or book that does the trick for you into an "Inspiration Library" document you can refer to at a moment's notice. Then latch onto them every time you need to drag yourself out of the dungeon of despair.

If it helps, here are a few selections from my Inspiration Library:

Movies
- It's a Wonderful Life
- Radio
- Bella
- Amazing Grace
- In America

Music
- Handel's "Messiah"
- Pachelbel's "Canon in D"
- Beethoven's 5th Symphony
- Beethoven's 9th Symphony
- Mozart's 41st Symphony
- Schubert's "Trout" Piano Quintet
- "O Holy Night"
- Schubert's "Ave Maria"
- "This is Your Life" by Switchfoot
- "Island in the Sun" by Weezer
- "Mint Car" by The Cure
- "Near Wild Heaven" by R.E.M.
- "I Was Here" by Beyoncé Knowles
- "I Was Here" by Lady Antebellum (yes, those are two different songs)

Books
- *A Million Miles in a Thousand Years* by Donald Miller
- *And There Was Light* by Jacques Lusseyran
- *Man's Search for Meaning* by Viktor Frankl
- *L.I.F.E.: Living Intentionally for Excellence* by Chris Brady & Orrin Woodward
- *Same Kind of Different as Me* by Ron Hall & Denver Moore
- *Up From Slavery* by Booker T. Washington
- *As a Man Thinketh* by James Allen
- *Loving What Is* by Byron Katie

WHAT'S IN *YOUR* INSPIRATION LIBRARY?

The Shameful Reason Why We Live Small

There are infinite ways to live big, but only one way to live small.

I was driving home one evening when I saw flashing lights from a barrage of police cars and emergency vehicles. They had closed the street off, necessitating a turn-around detour through the local rec center parking lot.

Annoyed, I thought, "They're not doing a good job of redirecting traffic. They need to have someone further up the road so we don't have to waste time turning around in this parking lot."

120

I drove home and tucked my four beautiful kids into bed, oblivious of the girl who would never be tucked in again.

The next morning Queen Karina said, "Did you hear about the twelve-year-old girl who was killed last night crossing the street in front of the rec center?"

Oh. My.

"Self-absorption in all its forms kills empathy, let alone compassion," says Daniel Goleman in his book, *Social Intelligence: The New Science of Human Relationships.* "When we focus on ourselves, our world contracts as our problems and preoccupations loom large. But when we focus on others, our world expands. Our own problems drift to the periphery of the mind and so seem smaller, and we increase our capacity for connection—or compassionate action."

Believe it or not, there are lives beyond our own, problems bigger than ours, pain worse than ours, burdens heavier than ours.

We don't need to have our pain alleviated, our burdens relieved. We simply need to put them into perspective by recognizing those of others. By doing so, our problems shrink and our vision and value to the world expand.

Forgetting about our own problems and helping other people solve theirs is the doorway to a life of meaning and greatness.

**Thoughtful, compassionate service is the key
that unlocks opportunity and unleashes joy.**

As Christ counseled, "Whosoever shall seek to save his life shall lose it; and whosoever shall lose his life shall preserve it."

Our energy can be spent whining about problems, or creating solutions. Our focus can be on meeting our own petty needs, or on relieving the heartache of others.

And that choice determines whether we live small or big.

Why Setting Goals

Failure is most often defined as not reaching one's goals. The imperative to set goals is found in virtually every self-help/success book.

"A fellow must know where he wants to go, if he is going to get anywhere," says Dr. William Menninger. "The people who go places and do things... know what they want and are willing to go an extra mile."

There is some truth to that, of course. But there's an even deeper truth that must be realized for goals to have any positive meaning or impact in our lives.

"I can teach anybody how to get what they want out of life," says Mark Twain. "The problem is that I can't find anybody who can tell me what they want."

Certainly, defining what we want—our goals—is fundamental to success. But even more fundamental is knowing not what we want, but *why* we want it. Truly successful people understand their "why" before striving for any "what."

Before we set goals, we must first develop a clear and authentic definition of success. Our worthy "whats" are determined by truthful "whys."

Achieving inauthentic goals does not constitute success. In fact, it's usually a more tragic failure than not achieving the right goals.

> *"For what shall it profit a man, if he shall gain the whole world, and lose his own soul?"*

What if our goals are misguided? What if they're the product of parroting imposed social scripts, rather than writing our own? What if, to paraphrase Stephen Covey, we climb our goal ladder only to find that we had leaned it against the wrong wall?

Are we pursuing material wealth because it's truly part of our personal, authentic definition of success, or because the message that wealth equates success is drilled into our brains from birth?

Can Be Dangerous

Worthy goals can only be determined after we've defined success for us individually. No one wants a drill; we want a hole, or what a drill can do for us. A goal is a drill. But what are your "holes"? What do you want your goals to do for you, or for the world?

For example, I had a goal to publish this book (drill). But what I really wanted is to help others exercise their power of choice more wisely—to think, dream, learn, do, and become more (hole). In other words, the goal of publishing a book is secondary to my definition of a successful outcome. Goals are simply means to greater ends.

Our definition of success determines which goals are worthy of our purpose and which are misguided, inauthentic distractions. Any time we change our definition of success, the goals we pursue and how we achieve them also changes drastically.

All too often we feel like failures when we compare ourselves to others. But this feeling does not come because we haven't achieved the same goals as other people. Rather, it comes because we've failed to define our own success and have bought into their definition. Envy is the result of not being in tune with who we are, what God wants us to do and become, what we were born to accomplish.

For example, you may envy a young millionaire. But if you knew his wealth was earned at the expense of his family, would you really want to trade places with him? Does he really have what you want?

Envy dissolves when we define success for ourselves, as based on 1) an intimate relationship with and firm allegiance to God, and 2) an authentic understanding of our unique gifts, passions, values, and purpose.

Failure is not falling short of one's goals. It is the result of pursuing the wrong goals for the wrong reasons.

THE HIDDEN GOLDMINE OF SELF-IMPROVEMENT

Goldmines in business are discovered by entrepreneurs who listen to complaints. For those who tap those complaint veins, by building businesses that solve problems, the payoff can be spectacular.

Likewise, we can discover the most lucrative goldmine in ourselves and tap the vein of our awesome personal power by paying attention to criticism. But where marketplace complaints reveal goldmines, the criticism I speak of is designed specifically to hide our goldmine of self-improvement.

For those with the courage and honesty to dig through deep layers of self-deception, the payoff is spectacular.

Want to strike gold and become rich in ability, character, credibility, leadership, and impact? Absorb, accept, and apply this uncomfortable, yet astoundingly empowering truth: **Our greatest source of self-improvement is found in our criticisms of others.**

Jungian psychology teacher Edward Whitmont explains, "Ask someone to give a description of the personality type which he finds most despicable, most unbearable and hateful, and most impossible to get along with, and he will produce a description of his own repressed characteristics...These very qualities are so unacceptable to him precisely because they represent his own repressed side; only that which we cannot accept within ourselves do we find impossible to live with in others."

Criticism reveals more about the criticizer than the target. We tell ourselves stories about other people to hide our most uncomfortable secrets from ourselves. As Dieter F. Uchtdorf says, "We often justify our anger and satisfy our consciences by telling ourselves stories about the motives of others that condemn their actions as unforgivable and egoistic while, at the same time, lifting our own motives as pure and innocent."

The more we criticize others, the more work we have to do on ourselves. To paraphrase Christ, the beams dragging us down are revealed as we pick at the slivers in the lives of others. The beams of our weaknesses provide the raw elements for building a life worth emulating—if we recognize them by being honest with ourselves.

But as we focus on our weaknesses, let us not forget that the purpose is not to tear ourselves down, but to build ourselves up. As Abraham Lincoln taught, "He has a right to criticize, who has a heart to help."

Those who criticize the most are building the least. Criticism is a luxury reserved for those unwilling to do anything worth criticizing. As Theodore Roosevelt proclaimed, "It is not the critic who counts: not the man who points out how the strong man stumbles or where the doer of deeds could have done better. The credit belongs to the man who is actually in the arena, whose face is marred by dust and sweat and blood, who strives valiantly, who errs and comes up short again and again, because there is no effort without error or shortcoming, but who knows the great enthusiasms, the great devotions, who spends himself for a worthy cause; who, at the best, knows, in the end, the triumph of high achievement, and who, at the worst, if he fails, at least he fails while daring greatly, so that his place shall never be with those cold and timid souls who knew neither victory nor defeat."

As we throw ourselves into a worthy cause, our weaknesses are quickly revealed. As we keep striving valiantly, we eventually overcome our weaknesses.

Every time we criticize others, our internal self-improvement detector screams that we've struck gold. But we can't hear it if we're not honest with ourselves. We can spend our lives either combing through the trash heap of others' weaknesses, or cashing in on the goldmine of self-improvement.

Divine Assurance for Those in Pain & Struggling

I watch it happen and my heart stops.

I am upstairs looking out the window onto the street. My seven-year-old daughter, Libby, comes tearing down the street on her Razor scooter. Her front tire hits a rock and her scooter stops cold. She does not stop.

And when she comes up screaming, my gut tells me it's going to be bad.

I bolt and streak down the stairs and barrel out the door. She is holding her left arm and howling. One look and I know.

We jump into the car and race to the hospital. The whole ride there, she wails that she can't take it anymore, frantically pleads with me to make it stop.

She is not the only one crying in agony. I would give anything to take her pain.

Now, flash back to three months earlier.

I am lying in a strange bed, alone and acutely lonely, at six o'clock in the morning, writhing in pain from a herniated disc in my back. I haven't slept all night, nor will I sleep more than two hours a night for the next month. I am 165 miles away from my family at a friend's house, a chiropractor who is helping me with therapy.

I beg my Father to make it stop. Through sobs, I tell Him I can't take it anymore.

The pain torments me for two bed-ridden months before I am forced to get surgery. Through the whole agonizing ordeal, I wonder if there's anyone watching me, who knows what I'm going through and who cares.

And as I helplessly watch my precious little girl bawling in a hospital bed, so afraid and in so much pain, *I know*.

This I know: We have a Father in Heaven who knows us better than we know ourselves. He loves us, cares for us, cherishes us, agonizes over us more than we can comprehend.

He knows the most intimate details of our lives. He understands what we're going through.

His heart breaks when He sees us in pain. He would take it for us, but He knows that we need it to make us strong, wise, compassionate. And He wants us to fully understand and experience joy—the joy that can only be known when we have also known suffering.

Through all our challenges and trials, we can know with absolute certainty that He is watching over us, He will come to our aid, He will give us strength and hope to endure.

And we can trust that He will make it all better.

HOW TO
FIGHT ENTROPY
AND NEVER STOP
PROGRESSING

IN Orson Scott Card's phenomenal fantasy series, *Tales of Alvin Maker*, the main antagonist is a supernatural force called the "Unmaker."

A character in the series explains, "It's the enemy of everything that exists. All it wants is to break everything into pieces, and break those pieces into pieces, until there's nothing left at all." Essentially, it is entropy as a conscious and unimaginably destructive force.

I believe in the Unmaker. But less as a supernatural, external force, and more as a fundamental component of human nature. It is inside us. And without constant vigilance, it will destroy us.

Entropy is hard-wired into the DNA of the human experience. Unused muscles get flabby. Unrestrained diets lead to obesity and disease. Uncontrolled thoughts spiral into negativity and degeneracy. Careless words erode relationships.

We are either progressing or declining. There is no middle ground. Mediocrity is more than stagnation—it is decay.

So how can we conquer entropy and cultivate perpetual progress in our lives? Three specific ways: At any given time we should have:

1. A TRANSFORMATIONAL BOOK TO READ.

2. A BURNING CURIOSITY TO SATISFY.

3. A SIGNIFICANT CREATION TO MANIFEST.

A TRANSFORMATIONAL BOOK TO READ

I'm not talking about light summer reading purely for entertainment. I'm talking about books that expand your mind, enrich your soul, transform your perspective, and motivate you to strive for excellence. Books that make you more conscious, more compassionate, more capable. Profound, multi-faceted, timeless books that can be read over and over again, with new lessons being gleaned each time.

Are you engrossed in such a book now? What's next on your list? Do you spend more time reading than watching TV?

A BURNING CURIOSITY TO SATISFY

The more books you read, the more curious you will become about an increasingly broad range of interests. For the progressing person, questions proliferate exponentially in proportion to answers received.

For example, one of my most recent curiosities was sparked by a years-long study of brain lateralization. For months I wondered if our subconscious mind was the same as the right hemisphere of our brain. My question was finally answered, the itch scratched, by reading *The Right Brain and the Unconscious* by Dr. R. Joseph.

Currently, I'm enthralled by the relationship between light and color.

What are you deeply curious about? What specific topic are you studying right now? What intellectual conundrum are you chewing on? What profound question are you trying to answer? What monumental puzzle are you trying to solve?

A SIGNIFICANT CREATION TO MANIFEST

The Unmaker is embedded in your soul. But strangely, so is its archenemy: your creative power. Your progress is measured by the depth, breadth, reach, and impact of your creative endeavors.

Creating anything of lasting value is a function of:

- **Vision:** Seeing clearly in your mind something that doesn't currently exist.
- **Action:** Taking baby steps toward achieving grandiose visions.
- **Commitment:** The willingness to give up anything and everything—your life, if necessary—to make your vision a reality.

What are you creating? A family? A business? A book? A work of art? How clear is your vision of what you want to create? What action are you taking to manifest that creation? How committed are you to your creation?

As Roy H. Williams would ask, what are you trying to make happen, and how will you measure success? Are you just dreaming about ideas and yapping about goals, or are you actually building something worthwhile?

The Unmaker scoffs at cheap talk. But he shrinks in fear from those who take conscious, consistent, dedicated action.
So tell me whether or not you have:

- A TRANSFORMATIONAL BOOK TO READ
- A BURNING CURIOSITY TO SATISFY
- A SIGNIFICANT CREATION TO MANIFEST

...and I will predict your future.
For those are the enemies of entropy and the fuels of progress.

WHY THOROUGH PREPARATION TRUMPS SPORADIC EMOTION

Everyone loves heart-stirring, blood-pumping halftime speeches in sports movies. The team is outmatched, whipped, down for the count. Spirits are crushed, heads hang low, tails are tucked between tired legs. Then, the coach reaches deep into his champion's heart to pull out a rip-roaring speech.

The fog of defeat is pierced by the sun of encouragement. Heads lift and begin to nod, spirits are aroused, and soon the team is shouting their conviction that victory is theirs. Refocused and rejuvenated, they charge the field and win the day.

Halftime emotionalism may make for good Hollywood drama. But true champions never depend on it to win.

That's according to John Wooden, by far the most successful coach in the history of basketball. Consider:

- **Wooden's UCLA teams won ten NCAA championships in twelve years, including seven in a row.**
- **He coached 88 consecutive victories, smashing the previous record of 60.**
- **His teams enjoyed eight undefeated Pacific conference crowns.**
- **His unprecedented lifetime winning percentage exceeded 80 percent.**

With that context, now ponder his counterintuitive insights into emotion, as revealed in his book, *Wooden: A Lifetime of Observations and Reflections On and Off the Court*:

> "I believe that for every artificial peak you create, there is a valley. I don't like valleys. Games are lost in valleys. Therefore, I wasn't much for giving speeches to stir up emotions before a game.
>
> "If you need emotionalism to make you perform better, then sooner or later you'll be vulnerable, an emotional wreck, and unable to function to your level of ability.
>
> "My ideal is an ever-rising graph line that peaks with your final performance.
>
> **"I prefer thorough preparation over some device to make us 'rise to the occasion.' Let others try to rise suddenly to a higher level than they had attained previously. We would have already attained it in our preparation. We would be there to begin with. A speech by me shouldn't be necessary."**

If your performance depends on stimulating your emotions at critical moments, something is wrong. It's not sustainable, and neither does it create long-term success.

Games are won long before you ever set foot on the court. You can't expect to hit homeruns if you rarely show up for batting practice. Larry Bird may have dreamed of holding an NBA championship trophy high under flashing lights. But while he was dreaming, he shot at least 500 free throws every day.

THE SUGARY HIGH OF SPORADIC EMOTIONS IS NOTHING COMPARED TO THE ENDURING NUTRITION OF PREPARATION. AND NO AMOUNT OF POSITIVE THINKING CAN COMPENSATE FOR INCOMPETENCE.

This is why I avoid personal development gurus who promise to "change your life" through "experiential" events. After the emotions stimulated by fast talkers, cheering crowds, and sleep deprivation have faded, what remains is the same person with the same skills, habits, and character. And those, like anything worthwhile, take years of sustained effort to develop.

So you can dream of glory or think as positively as you want. But when you show up to deliver a speech, close a sale, counsel a wayward youth, perform a surgery, or launch a business, the cold, hard truth is this: either you're ready or you're not. And no pep talk in the moment, no matter how heartfelt, will change that inescapable fact.

Be not deceived by charismatic charlatans or Hollywood drama. Your character is not forged from the sparks of "life-changing" weekends, but through the fires of daily choices over years. And championships are not won because of rousing halftime speeches. They're won because of years of hard practice.

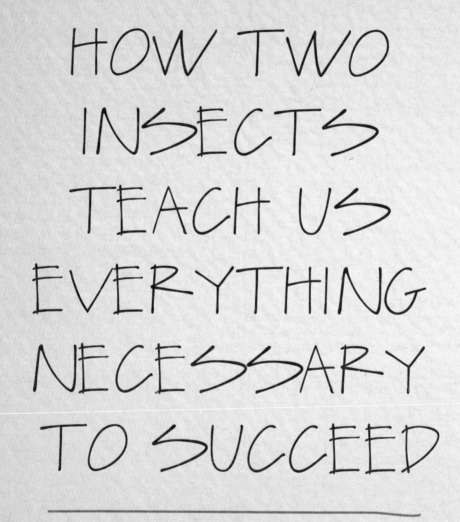

HOW TWO INSECTS TEACH US EVERYTHING NECESSARY TO SUCCEED

Old Aesop knew what he was talking about. According to his classic parable, there are two kinds of people: "ants" and "grasshoppers."

The slogan of the grasshoppers is, "The best things in life are free." The ants retort, "There's no such thing as a free lunch."

Grasshoppers live for today, spend more than they earn, rack up consumer debt, and spend selfishly on themselves. Ants live within their means, prepare for the future, and leave a legacy for future generations.

Grasshoppers dream; ants act. Grasshoppers wish; ants work. Grasshoppers wait for opportunity; ants create opportunity.

Grasshoppers depend on luck to succeed, and often whine about their lack of it. As Orison Swett Marden taught,

"It is the idle person, not the great worker, who is always complaining that there is no time or opportunity. Yet, some will make more out of the odds and ends of opportunities which many carelessly toss away than others will get out of a whole lifetime. Like bees, they extract honey from every flower. Every person they meet, every circumstance of the day, adds something to their store of useful knowledge or personal power."

Grasshoppers buy lottery tickets and speculate in the stock market. Ants create value for others and mitigate risk. Grasshoppers flit from one "ground floor" opportunity to another, without ever paying the price to succeed in any. Ants know their Soul Purpose and pursue it with laser focus and relentless determination.

Grasshoppers love prescription drugs and liposuction. Ants eat healthy food and exercise regularly.

Grasshoppers demand government benefits. Ants produce their own benefits. As B.J. Palmer put it,

"Men and women are of two kinds: floaters, who drift down stream like so much flotsam on the surface of the tide; like blood-suckers, they live off the efforts of those on whom they leech; and those who swim up stream, buck the tide of adversity, and struggle to support themselves as well as others."

Charismatic charlatans, offering quick, simple, and "revolutionary" life shortcuts, prey on grasshoppers, for grasshoppers provide their source of income. Grasshoppers are "like children, tossed to and fro, and carried about with every wind of doctrine, by the sleight of men, and cunning craftiness..."

Ants trust their own intuition and understand that building anything worthwhile requires hard work, time, and patience. Grasshoppers try "life-changing" techniques once or twice, then give up in disappointment.

Ants understand that change is a lifelong process, not a one-time event. They understand that virtue is achieved through total immersion in light and truth—that fighting entropy is not a periodic battle, but a constant war. As Henry David Thoreau observed,

> "As a single footstep will not make a path on the earth, so a single thought will not make a pathway in the mind. To make a deep physical path, we walk again and again. To make a deep mental path, we must think over and over the kind of thoughts we wish to dominate our lives."

Grasshoppers are enamored by any items new and shiny, then toss them out when they quickly get bored. Ants latch onto the things which endure. Grasshoppers are one-hit wonders. Ants create timeless classics.

The lives of grasshoppers are governed by whim, impulse, and emotion. They concern themselves little with potential consequences of their actions.

Ants are governed by natural laws, particularly the Law of the Harvest. They understand that a price must be paid to fulfill any desire, that consequences are inescapable and irrevocable.

The Proverb admonishes,

> "Go to the ant, thou sluggard! Consider her ways and be wise, which having no guide, overseer or ruler, provides her meat in the summer, and gathereth her food in the harvest."

OUR CHOICE IS TO CAVE TO OUR INNER GRASSHOPPER, OR CONSTANTLY STRIVE FOR THE IDEALS OF THE ANT.

Confessions of a Struggling Grasshopper

I have a confession: I've always struggled with my inner grasshopper.

Caught up in materialism, misguided by a "something-for-nothing" mindset, I once made boneheaded investment mistakes, which devastated my family financially for a time.

I've joined my share of "ground-floor" business opportunities, and quit and failed each after not paying the price.

I've fallen for the standard advertising tricks and racked up my share of consumer debt.

It took me a long time to find my purpose. Until I did, I floundered in dead-end jobs that weren't an expression of my truest self.

I've missed plenty of opportunities because of fear. I have fallen for deceitful shortcuts and suffered the consequences.

I've frequently fallen into the "someday" trap with my health—you know, "Someday I'll eat better and exercise more."

My articles are directed at myself more than anyone else. I write to articulate ideals, to which we can all aspire, notwithstanding our flaws. I echo the poignant words of Seneca, "I persist in praising not the life that I lead, but that which I ought to lead. I follow it at a mighty distance, crawling."

I'm passionate about articulating ideals because ideals inspire mankind to keep moving forward. They remind us of what's important and enduring.

Truth is, all of us have some grasshopper and some ant in us. We all struggle with weaknesses and temptations. What's important isn't where we are, but rather the direction in which we're headed.

Don't be discouraged by how far you fall short of ideals. The only cause for discouragement is when you give up pursuing them.

> Ideals should uplift and encourage you. If you ever feel discouraged by them, don't look at the road ahead of you and focus on how far you have to go. Look at the road behind you and see how far you've come.

It's healthy and productive to periodically and realistically take inventory of our progress (or lack thereof). But that's totally different than letting our inner critic dictate our moods.

So listen, fellow grasshopper: You and I are better today than we were yesterday. And with sincere and consistent effort, we'll be better tomorrow than we are today. We may not ever achieve perfection, but we can always progress.

THE ALARMING REASON WHY
I Flipped the Bird
IN SECOND GRADE

AS AN INNOCENT SECOND-GRADER, I WAS WALKING HOME FROM SCHOOL ONE DAY WITH A FRIEND. MY FRIEND DARED ME TO "FLIP THE BIRD" TO THE NEXT CAR THAT DROVE BY. IF I DID, HE PROMISED HE'D GIVE ME A PACK OF CANDY CIGARETTES.

NOT HAVING ANY IDEA WHAT IT MEANT, BUT ONLY HOW TO DO IT, I DID INDEED FLIP THE BIRD. CANDY CIGARETTES WERE ON THE LINE, AFTER ALL.

AND THE CAR PROMPTLY PULLED OVER. A MAN EMERGED. I WAS SCARED TO DEATH. IN NO UNCERTAIN TERMS AND WITH NO LACK OF VIGOR, HE TOLD ME JUST HOW IMPRESSED HE WAS WITH MY GESTURE. BUT THE REAL PUNISHMENT CAME AFTER HE WALKED ME HOME AND TOLD MY PARENTS WHAT I HAD DONE. AND TO TOP IT OFF, I NEVER COLLECTED ON MY BLASTED CANDY CIGARETTES.

TURNS OUT I'M NOT THE ONLY ONE WHO'S DONE BONEHEADED THINGS BECAUSE OF THE INFLUENCE OF FRIENDS (INCLUDING BEING TEMPTED BY CIGARETTES).

IN THE LIVE EXTRAORDINARY MANIFESTO (available at lifemanifestos.com) I WROTE,
"WHO YOU BECOME TOMORROW IS DETERMINED BY THE BOOKS YOU READ,
THE FRIENDS YOU KEEP, AND HOW YOU SPEND YOUR FREE TIME TODAY."

Gleaning insights from decades of research data, Harvard professors Nicholas Christakis and James Fowler have discovered the following, which they detail in their book *Connected: How Your Friends' Friends' Friends Affect Everything You Feel, Think, and Do*:

- We are 61 percent more likely to smoke if we have a direct relationship with a smoker. If your friend of a friend is a smoker, you are 29 percent more likely to smoke. Even at a third degree of separation (friend of a friend's friend), you are 11 percent more likely.

- If you have a friend that becomes obese, the odds that you'll gain weight jump to 57 percent.

- A British study revealed that among binge drinkers, 54 percent reported that all or almost all of their friends are binge drinkers, compared to 15 percent of non-binge drinkers.

- One Harvard study found that Harvard students were 8.3 percent more likely to get a flu shot if an additional 10 percent of their friends got a flu shot.

- People who are surrounded by happy people have a significantly greater likelihood of future happiness.

It's just common sense that we tend to mirror the attitudes, emotions, likes, interests, and habits of our peers—"birds of a feather" and all that. As social critic Eric Hoffer put it, "When people are free to do as they please, they usually imitate each other."

But underlying common sense is a fascinating biological mechanism in the human brain, which scientists call the "mirror neuron system." Christakis and Fowler explain:

"Our brains practice doing actions we merely observe in others, as if we were doing them ourselves. If you've ever watched an intense fan at a game, you know what we are talking about — he twitches at every mistake, aching to give his own motor actions to the players on the field.

"When we see players run, jump, or kick, it is not only our visual cortex or even the part of our brain that thinks about what we are observing that is activated, but also the parts of our brain that would be activated if we ourselves were running, jumping, or kicking...

"It seems we are always poised to feel what others feel and do what others do."

W. Clement Stone was not exaggerating when he said, "Be careful the environment you choose for it will shape you; be careful the friends you choose for you will become like them." That's why Thomas J. Watson counseled, "Don't make friends who are comfortable to be with. Make friends who will force you to lever yourself up."

Whether we flip the bird for candy cigarettes or strive for greatness,
the influence our friends have on our decisions, actions, and habits
cannot be underestimated.

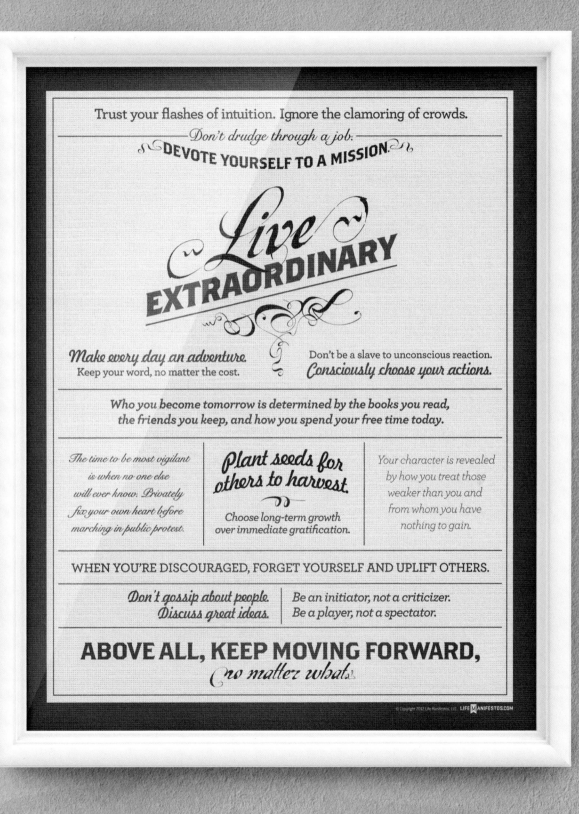

Life-Changing Truths Gleaned from a Misleading U-Haul Sticker

"Speed kills."

I read that sticker on the dashboard of a U-Haul truck countless times as I drove 1,236 miles to move my family. As the miles and hours passed over two days, I pondered the phrase.

Wax philosophical with me for a moment. This is important.

Technically, I concluded, speed does not kill. What kills is the loss of blood and function from fatal impact. Speed can certainly be a causal factor for accidents, which can cause fatal impact. But if you're going to blame death on one causal factor, why not move further up the causal chain?

Can we not just as easily say, "Driving kills"? And why stop there? What causes us to drive? In my case, my family and I decided to move. Does moving kill, because we drive to move and we may speed while driving? And what about the factors that led to our decision to move, the causal factors set in motion long before we ever got on the road to move? If we can blame death on one causal factor, we can logically blame it on any causal factor—none of which are technically true causes.

Here's what *is* true: Choices and actions bear consequences.
Wise people learn to foresee consequences and act accordingly.

SAYS WISE MAN VIKTOR FRANKL,

"Live as if you were living already for the second time and as if you had acted the first time as wrongly as you are about to act now."

Read that quote again, will you? And a third time, slowly and carefully. Let it really sink in. *It is one of the most important quotes you will ever read in your life.*

Live as if you could foresee the consequences of your actions.

Saying "Speed kills" is like saying "Infidelity causes divorce." But what causes infidelity? What will be the long-term consequences of how you treat your spouse today? What can you say to or do for your spouse today that will bear the fruits of love and joy decades from now? Live as if you were living already for the second time and as if you had seen what happens to your marriage as a result of how you treat your spouse today.

If we say, "Speed kills," we can also say that addiction ruins lives. But trace addiction up the causal chain and you ultimately arrive at one choice in a portentous moment. One indulgent moment leading to another and another, character and willpower eroding with each choice.

What are you putting into your mind and body today, and what will that ultimately cause? As my friend Kris Krohn says, "I don't have to stick my head in a garbage can to know it stinks."

Live as if you were already living for the second time and as if you had stuck your head in the garbage can the first time. You know it stinks. How does this change your choices today?

Every thought, every choice, every act is a seed. Seeds take root and bear fruit. Ultimately, there are only two kinds of fruit: misery and joy. Misery seeds are deceiving because they feel good when they are planted. Live as if you were living already for the second time and as if you had seen the fruits of the seeds you are about to plant now.

Indulgence may feel good now, but how will it feel later? Sacrifice may be tough now, but what will it produce later?

Speed doesn't kill. But it does, like all our actions, carry consequences.

HOW THINKING INSIDE THE BOX MAKES US MORE

CREATIVE

"THINKING OUTSIDE THE BOX," WE'VE BEEN TOLD, IS THE PATH TO BOUNDLESS CREATIVITY AND RECORD-SHATTERING INNOVATION.

IN FACT, IT IS PRECISELY LIMITATIONS AND CONSTRAINTS THAT SPARK OUR MOST CREATIVE IDEAS AND GENERATE THE MOST PRACTICAL AND INNOVATIVE SOLUTIONS. OUR CONSTRAINTS HOLD THE KEY TO OUR FREEDOM.

Consider an exercise:

For which of the following two challenges could you generate the most practical, implementable ideas in ten minutes?

1. **Create a business.**
2. **Create an online business that:**
   - Leverages your particular interests and passions (the more clearly defined, the better)
   - Requires no more than $1,000 to start.
   - Can be operated in ten hours per week or less.
   - Can eventually generate at least $2,000 net profit per month.

> **"When forced to work within a strict framework, the imagination is taxed to its utmost and will produce its richest ideas."**
>
> -T.S. Eliot

The first challenge has no box, no defined limitations. And that's precisely why we draw a blank. Or, the exercise may spark interesting ideas, but the vast majority of them are worthless and unworkable.

Creativity doesn't simply mean having an abundance of ideas. It means actually creating concrete, useful solutions that create value in the world.

The second challenge is a clearly-defined box, which is exactly why it engages our imagination and sparks practical ideas much more easily.

This is what Ernie Schenck calls the "Houdini Solution" in his empowering book, *The Houdini Solution: Put Creativity and Innovation to Work by Thinking Inside the Box.* Houdini was successful, says Schenck, because he accepted his self-imposed limitations and worked within their confines. His straitjackets, chains, ropes, locks, coffins didn't hold him captive—in fact, they defined his success.

Writes Schenck, "[Houdini] accepted the box. He accepted the water inside the box. He accepted the chains and the locks. Rather than allowing his mind to be consumed with the problem, he directed all of his energy toward solving it."

Like Houdini's chains, we have inescapable constraints in our business or job, our marriage, our relationships, our physical abilities—in virtually every aspect of our lives. We can spend our lives bemoaning our fate, or we can accept our limitations and work within them to become more creative, innovative, and successful than we ever could have been without them.

Nick Vujicic was born with no arms or legs. Rather than lounging on the couch dreaming of flying, he waddles on stumps onto stages and wows crowds with his indomitable spirit.

As Ernie Schenck reveals: "The biggest secret of truly productive creative people is that they embrace obstacles, they don't run from them. In their minds every setback is an opportunity, every limitation is a chance. Where others see a wall, they see a doorway."

If we can't recognize and accept our constraints, we'll be forever enslaved by them. Ironically, only by embracing them will solutions arise.

> **"Creativity requires limits, for the creative act arises out of the struggle of human beings and against that which limits them."**
>
> -Rollo May

But our "box" is defined by more than constraints. It's also defined by assets. In fact, accepting our constraints helps us recognize assets we haven't seen before.

> **"What I wouldn't give for a holocaust cloak."**
>
> -Wesley on The Princess Bride, when faced with the challenge of defeating sixty men with three

Potential assets remain unrecognized, unvalued, and unleveraged until we're forced into a corner. This is why so many heroic entrepreneurs have emerged during this recession. They've taken a hard look at their circumstances. They've accepted the constraints imposed by a crashed economy. They've played the hand they were dealt, rather than folding in despair.

Life will never deal us a full house. Instead, it's given us a box with tough constraints. But within the framework of those constraints—and the assets they reveal—is the key to our freedom.

WHAT TO DO WHEN YOUR BACK IS AGAINST THE WALL

LIFE IS LIKE A GAME OF SCRABBLE. AND THERE WAS A TIME IN MY LIFE WHEN I WAS STARING AT AN EMPTY BOARD WITH A HANDFUL OF LOUSY LETTERS.

In late 2007, Queen Karina and I were heavily invested in real estate. We were banking on a 7,500 square foot house paying us $250,000 after finishing the basement. Then the housing bubble burst, and our plans along with it. We were extremely lucky to sell the house and break even. We negotiated to live for six months in the basement we had just paid a lot of money to finish.

We ended up losing five properties, $120,000 cash, our car, most of our furniture, and most importantly, our main source of income.

Soon after we had moved into the basement, I discovered that our bank account would be overdrawn if I didn't act fast. I had no income and not a clue as to what to do.

I hit my knees. After a long time, an idea emerged. I had an asset that could be leveraged. A paltry, insignificant little thing, to be sure. But something to work with.

The previous year I had made an audio recording of a few essays (many of which would later be published in my book, *Uncommon Sense: A Common Citizen's Guide to Rebuilding America*). I had a box full of CDs sitting in a closet.

I arose, dressed nice, and hit the streets to sell my CD door-to-door. That silly little CD put food on my family's table and paid our bills for a couple months. (Would you believe I made $33.40 an hour selling it? True story—I kept meticulous records, which I still have.)

Queen Karina and I like to play Scrabble. Occasionally we'll catch each other bemoaning our letters, saying, "If only I had an 's,'" or whichever letter we need to score big. We remind each other to play the board—to play what *is*, not what we wish for.

"If only" is an absurd waste of time and energy. In Scrabble, as in life, we can wish for something different all we want. But our board is our board, our letters are our letters. We got what we got, and no amount of wishing or whining will change that. We must forget what we don't have, focus on what we do have, and play what we can.

Theodore Roosevelt put it like this: "Do what you can, with what you have, where you are."

Sometimes in life we draw lousy letters and we're staring at an empty board. What we do in those moments defines us and determines whether or not we'll be prepared when everything falls into place. If we bemoan our fate and whine "if only" when our letters are lousy, we'll still be whining when they're fabulous and we won't see and capitalize on opportunity.

And more often than not, the letters we think are lousy can actually score big.

One time I was staring at these letters on a tough Scrabble board: I V R I I L T. I cursed the letters and played something lame for nine points, only to discover that I could have played "virility," using all my letters for seventy-two points.

If we focus on abundance and possibility, assets and opportunities are revealed that we can't see when we're focused on what we wish we had.

We see what we want to see. What we see determines what we do. What we do determines the results we experience.

The faster we accept reality, the better we play the game of life. Forget what you wish you had. Play what you have. Because it's better than you think.

Mr. Incredible, you'll recall, arrives home from work one day to find the neighbor kid lurking on his tricycle in the Incredibles' driveway.

"What are *you* waiting for?" Mr. Incredible demands.

"I dunno," shrugs the kid. "Something a*maz*ing, I guess."

That wishful statement from a cartoon boy reveals profound insights into human nature. It explains why millions of people lurk at magazine racks gawking at celebrities in cheap tabloids. Amazing, isn't it, how much time people will spend watching other people be amazing? Fearful and unwilling to live an outstanding life themselves, they get their fix of amazing vicariously.

The kid's comment also explains why I closed all my personal social media accounts. I found that too often, when mentally blocked and uninspired, I would lurk on Facebook waiting for something amazing to happen.

Are *you* lurking on the sidelines of life waiting for something amazing to happen?

*a*mazing doesn't just happen. You have to make it happen. Opportunity ships never come in while you're lazing on the beach, gazing wistfully at the horizon. You have to build them yourself, turn your back to land, and set sail.

The passive life is the entropic life — which is to say a life squandered and tainted by regret. The only honorable form of waiting is that of working in your daily trenches, building the foundations of your greatness.

As Longfellow concludes his classic poem, "A Psalm of Life":

> *Let us, then, be up and doing,*
> *With a heart for any fate;*
> *Still achieving, still pursuing,*
> *Learn to labor and to wait.*

The most amazing accomplishments take time and patience to build. Fireworks and cathedrals are both amazing, but one is gone in a flash and the other lasts for centuries.

And while you're building your amazing magnum opus, never forget that you're enveloped in amazing miracles every mundane moment of every day. While dreaming of grand adventures, never miss the ones right in front of your nose.

Remember how Bob Parr, fed up with the drudgery of his insurance job, tries to relive his Mr. Incredible days by doing covert hero work at night? His wife, Helen (Elastigirl), pleads with him, "Yes, [the glory days] happened. But this—our family—is what's happening now, Bob. And you are missing this!"

With discerning eyes and an attuned heart, playing and laughing with your family is more amazing than an expedition to the pyramids on the back of a camel.

Living a life of amazement usually takes more quiet gratitude than intense striving. It's more about attitude than action.

But make no mistake — your actions will dramatically impact your attitude. As Roy H. Williams advises, "If you will expand your world, you must crawl on your hands and knees, get on your belly and squirm under the fence that surrounds your insulated life."

So drive a different way to work. Go home and dance with your spouse and tickle your kids. Wake up early and marvel at the sunrise. Take that trip to South America you've been dreaming of. Act on that inspiration to develop that product. Write that book that's weighing on your heart.

Take nothing for granted. Live extraordinary. Be incredible and make amazing happen.

INSPIRATIONAL LIFE MANIFESTOS

I founded Life Manifestos (LifeManifestos.com) to create inspirational manifesto posters designed as works of art to resonate with people who strive for excellence and significance.

The manifestos are your planted flag, your line in the sand, your standard held high.

They are predicated upon the firm belief that words and art can change the world. As people display these in their homes and offices—bold proclamations to a jaded and complacent world—new conversations arise. Principles, ideas, and ideals are considered, discussed, and debated in ways they never would have otherwise.

They poetically and profoundly express the essence of who you are, what you believe, and what you stand for. They are constant reminders to always strive for improvement, follow your bliss, to make a difference.

Get 25 percent off your next order by using the coupon code MANIFESTDESTINY at checkout.

(One time use, may not be combined with other offers).

MANIFESTOS FOR PURCHASE

The following Life Manifestos are available as posters and canvas prints at LifeManifestos.com.

WE ARE BEST FRIENDS.

In our home you are *loved* wanted, appreciated, and cherished—no matter what. **You are safe to be vulnerable.** To be silly. To vent your frustrations. To share your emotions, struggles, and embarrassments. We encourage you to ◆ *We give you confidence to* **dream BIG,** **WE ARE** ◆ **Family** *venture into the world and get knocked down.* and we do everything possible to make your dreams come true. *Come back to us.*

◆ **WE COMFORT, HEAL, AND STRENGTHEN YOU.** ◆

And whisk you back out the door with a smile on your face, the dream glistening in your eyes, courage beating in your heart. ◆ **WE BELIEVE in you.** We're on your team. In your corner. Your biggest fans. Cheering our hearts out for you to reach, strive, leave it all on the field, **become who you were born to become.** *We are family: united, unbreakable, eternal.*

Family Manifesto
16" x 20"

Trust your flashes of intuition. Ignore the clamoring of crowds.

— *Don't drudge through a job.* —

DEVOTE YOURSELF TO A MISSION.

Live **EXTRAORDINARY**

Make every day an adventure.
Keep your word, no matter the cost.

Don't be a slave to unconscious reaction.
Consciously choose your actions.

*Who you become tomorrow is determined by the books you read,
the friends you keep, and how you spend your free time today.*

*The time to be most vigilant
is when no one else
will ever know. Privately
fix your own heart before
marching in public protest.*

*Plant seeds for
others to harvest*

Choose long-term growth
over immediate gratification.

*Your character is revealed
by how you treat those
weaker than you and
from whom you have
nothing to gain.*

WHEN YOU'RE DISCOURAGED, FORGET YOURSELF AND UPLIFT OTHERS.

*Don't gossip about people.
Discuss great ideas.*

Be an initiator, not a criticizer.
Be a player, not a spectator.

ABOVE ALL, KEEP MOVING FORWARD,
no matter what.

Live Extraodinary Manifesto

16" x 20"

■ Poster   ■ Canvas

Leave a Legacy

LEAVE SOMETHING WHEN YOU DIE.

A tree planted. A garden cultivated. A wound healed. A book written. A child taught.

Be a sculptor. **LEAVE YOUR FINGERPRINTS ON THE HEARTS OF THOSE YOU TOUCH.**

Be an artist, not a wage earner. A linchpin, not a laborer.

No matter your station, no matter the job.

If you're a janitor, don't sweep floors and empty trash—sparkle the world with cleanliness, order, and beauty.

If you're a mason, don't look to the ground and chisel rocks—gaze at the sky and build cathedrals.

Act ON YOUR **INSPIRATIONS.**

NEVER BE CONTENT WITH THE STATUS QUO—FIGHT IT WITH A RELENTLESS PASSION FOR EXCELLENCE.

Leave it all on the field of life.

YOU CAN LIE IN YOUR DEATHBED TORTURED BY "IF ONLY'S" *or rest with the assurance that* **THE WORLD IS BETTER BECAUSE YOU LIVED.**

GO. LIVE. DO. BE. LEAVE A LEGACY.

I am Grateful

I BEGIN EACH DAY BY GIVING THANKS FOR TEN THINGS IN MY LIFE, PONDERING WHAT MY LIFE WOULD BE WITHOUT EACH.

I TAKE NOTHING FOR GRANTED. I MARVEL AT COMMON MIRACLES: THE NEWBORN BABY, THE GROWING SEED, EVERY BEAT OF MY HEART.

WHEN I FEEL ANGRY, FRUSTRATED, OR DISCOURAGED, I COUNT MY BLESSINGS UNTIL I FEEL **PEACE AND JOY.**

WHEN LIFE DOES NOT MEET MY EXPECTATIONS, I THANK GOD FOR THE PRIVILEGE OF GROWTH AND **FIND THE OPPORTUNITIES THAT LIE HIDDEN WITHIN DISAPPOINTMENTS.**

WHEN FACED WITH TRIALS, I REMEMBER THAT, AS GOLD IS EXTRACTED FROM ORE THROUGH FIRE, IT IS ONLY THROUGH TRIALS THAT I AM PURIFIED.

WHEN I SEE PEOPLE STRUGGLING AND IN PAIN, I THANK GOD FOR MY OWN STRUGGLES, WHICH HAVE GIVEN ME EYES TO SEE AND INCREASED MY DESIRE AND CAPACITY TO UPLIFT OTHERS.

MY CONSCIOUS, PERSISTENT GRATITUDE IS THE CATALYST FOR COMPASSIONATE SERVICE, AND THE FRUIT OF SERVICE IS JOY.

I WILL BE EVER MINDFUL OF THE NEEDS OF OTHERS, AND

I will be joyful.

I produce more value than I consume.

I reject complacency, mediocrity, conformity, and dependency.

I am a PRODUCER

I am not held captive by fear. I am fueled by vision and passion, governed by principles, guided by ideals. I do not succeed through luck, but through conscious effort. I am not entitled to the fruit of another man's labor. My results are my responsibility. I am not a victim of circumstance. I am a victor by choice. I live by design, not by default. I seek not the stale comfort of a safe harbor, but the thrill of the open sea.

While others complain about problems, I create solutions and opportunities.

I see abundance where others see scarcity. I am relentlessly innovative. I do not wait for "someday" happiness; I choose happiness now. I am not afraid to act and fail; failure is simply accelerated learning.

I trust my inner voice over popular opinion.

While others gnaw on the bones of security, I feast on the meat of freedom.

While others criticize from couches and demonstrate in streets, I toil in trenches.
While others are blaming, I'm busy building.

I am a Producer

Producer Manifesto

18" x 24"

■ Poster   ■ Canvas

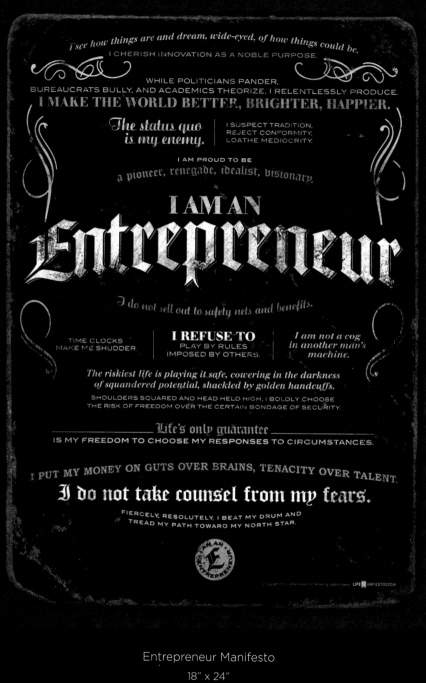

Entrepreneur Manifesto

18" x 24"
■ Poster   ■ Canvas

OUR HOME IS FILLED WITH HIS LIGHT BECAUSE WE LEARN OF HIM.

OUR HEARTS ARE FILLED WITH
HIS LOVE BECAUSE WE FOLLOW HIM.

WE BELIEVE IN
Christ

HE IS OUR EXALTED SAVIOR TO WHOM WE OWE EVERYTHING.

AND HE IS OUR DEAREST FRIEND
WITH WHOM WE CAN SHARE EVERYTHING.

WHEN WE ARE WEARY
WE FEEL HIM
BEARING
OUR BURDENS,
AND WE ARE STRENGTHENED.

WHEN WE CRY OUT IN AGONY
WE FEEL HIS TENDER
ARMS AROUND US,
AND WE FIND COMFORT AND HOPE.

WHEN WE ARE FEARFUL
WE HEAR HIS
ENCOURAGING VOICE,
AND WE ARE FILLED
WITH PEACE AND POWER.

*When we are wounded we remember His wounds,
and we forgive and are healed.*

AS HE WILL NEVER ABANDON US, NEITHER WILL WE EVER DENY HIM.
WE REMEMBER HIM, WE TRUST IN HIM, WE STRIVE TO BE LIKE HIM.

Creator Manifesto

I wrote the Creator Manifesto to complement and accompany the book
The Conscious Creator: Six Laws for Manifesting Your Masterpiece Life, which
I co-authored with Kris Krohn (www.Liberty.Strongbrook.com).

Written as a story, the book helps you:

- Overcome unconscious forces and live as a Conscious Creator.
- Alter your perceptions of reality and move from victim to victor.
- Become more creative, innovative, and productive.
- Gain clarity on exactly what you want to do and be -- to live by design, rather than default.
- Increase your faith and personal power to achieve your goals.
- Uncover and uproot false and limiting beliefs, and replace them with true and empowering beliefs.
- Make more money by living your passion.
- Create and manifest the life of your dreams, and leave a lasting legacy.

Download a free sample and purchase the book at
LifeManifestos.com. Save 15 percent by purchasing the
book with the Creator Manifesto as a package deal,
which you'll find under "Book + Manifesto Packages"
on the website.

www.Liberty.Strongbrook.com

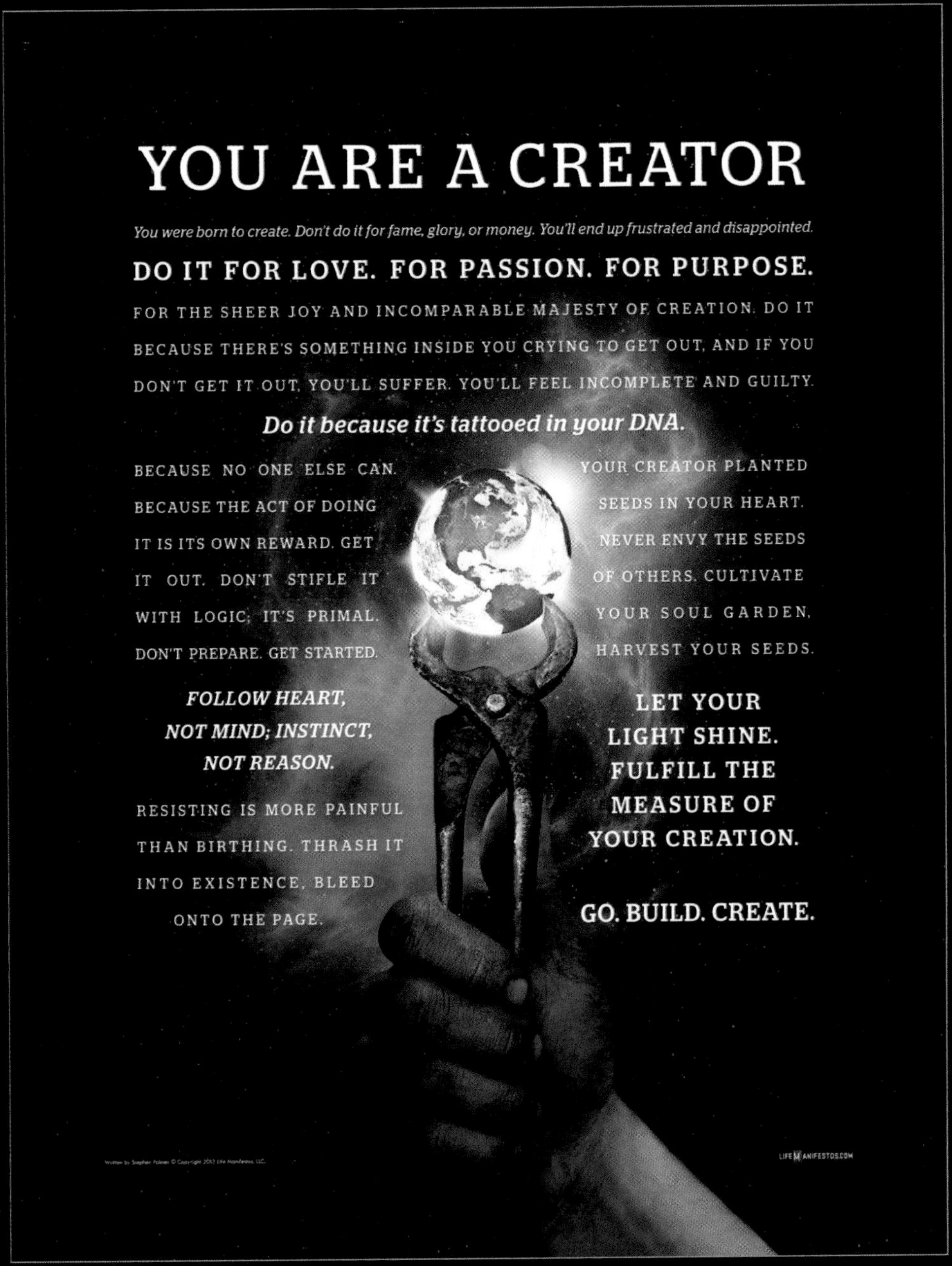

Creator Manifesto

18" x 24"

■ Poster ■ Canvas

Leadership Education Manifesto

The Leadership Education Manifesto was created as a collaborative effort between me and Oliver and Rachel DeMille, the developers of Leadership Education, also known as Thomas Jefferson Education.

Leadership Education is an educational philosophy and a methodology by which great individuals throughout history have been educated.

Using classic works, mentors, and the "7 Keys of Great Teaching," the purpose of the methodology is to help students discover, develop, and polish their genius to impact the world.

Learn more about Leadership Education by exploring TJEd.org and by reading *A Thomas Jefferson Education* by Oliver DeMille.

The Leadership Education Manifesto is available as a package deal with the book at 15 percent off at LifeManifestos.com.

www.tjed.org

An Education
To Match Our Mission

A MOVEMENT *is* SWEEPING *across the* WORLD.
Not of PROTESTORS *raging in streets.* BUT *of* FAMILIES
LOVING *and* LEARNING *in* CONSECRATED HOMES.

Of devoted mothers who look into their children's eyes and see future leaders.

Of valiant fathers who thirst for greatness.

OF YOUTH WHO FEEL A STIRRING IN THEIR SOULS TO RENOUNCE CONVEYOR-BELT MEDIOCRITY.

They HEAR *the* CALL *of* MISSION *to* SEEK TRUTH, BUILD STRONG FAMILIES *and communities,* SPREAD FREEDOM *and* PROSPERITY, *create beauty,* HEAL SOCIETY.

THEIR ALLEGIANCE IS CLEAR.

They will not compromise their virtue. They will not rest while they see need.

THEY UNPLUG FROM TELEVISION AND TABLOIDS TO IMMERSE THEMSELVES IN THE CLASSICS AND ENGAGE WITH MENTORS.

They learn because they are
INSPIRED,
NOT REQUIRED.

Compelled to grapple with life's most important questions. To earn a Leadership Education. To innovate solutions for humanity. To learn more, become more, so they can serve more.

We are this generation of leaders.

WE WILL RISE TO OUR POTENTIAL WITH
AN EDUCATION TO MATCH OUR MISSION.
And we will be the change we wish to see in the world.

Rascal Manifesto

The Rascal Manifesto was written by Chris Brady (www.ChrisBrady.com) and was first published in his book, *Rascal: Making a Difference by Becoming an Original Character.*

A co-founder of the Life Leadership company (www.Life-Leadership-Home.com), Chris explains that being a Rascal is a spirit of willfulness and strength, a dynamic force that drives one forward toward a unique path and contribution. It is character in motion, originality in broad relief, uniqueness for the sake of being true to oneself and one's cause. It is authenticity in courageous display. It is life lived on purpose and for a purpose.

Highlighting a number of Rascals throughout history, the book is a call to action to awaken Rascals everywhere. The world desperately needs people to get out of line and stand for absolute truths, and explains how the concepts of freedom and justice have always been won, defended, and passed along by Rascals.

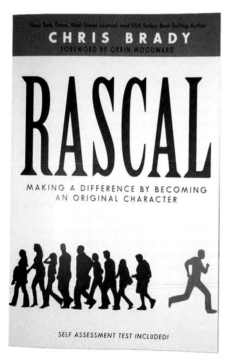

The Rascal Manifesto and book are both available for purchase at LifeManifestos.com. Purchase them together as a package deal to save 15 percent.

www.ChrisBrady.com
www.Life-Leadership-Home.com

I WAS BORN FREE AND I LIVE FREE.
NO ONE OWNS ME BUT MY CREATOR. *I am fiercely independent,*
and interdependent with those aligned in common purpose.
I KNOW FREEDOM COMES WITH RESPONSIBILITY.
I take responsibility for my actions. I HOLD
I AM NOT AFRAID TO STRUGGLE, THE BAR
FOR THAT HIGH
IS WHAT
MAKES ME ON MYSELF.
GREAT. I know
I AM A excellence
lies on the
LEARNING other side of
MACHINE. inconvenience.

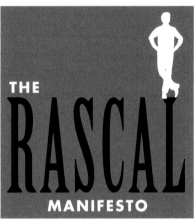

I read, I confront brutal reality, I grow.
I CANNOT BE DEFEATED. I learn the principles of freedom,
I KEEP COMING BACK, and strive to preserve freedom
STRONGER AND BETTER, for future generations.
NO MATTER WHAT. *I rely on no man or government to provide for me.*
I DO NOT FOLLOW THE HERD.
I RUN WITH A PACK OF RASCALS. I DEFY TYRANNY. I CHARGE THE HILL.
I MAKE A DIFFERENCE. **I AM A RASCAL.**

Rascal Manifesto
18" x 24"
■ Poster   ■ Canvas

Obstaclés Manifesto

Created by Chris Brady, the Obstaclés character represents all the obstacles we face in life, whether from our personal weaknesses or from external circumstances.

Obstaclés is relentless in his quest to bring Rascals down. But that undermining weasel is no match for heroic Rascals who know their purpose, maintain a firm allegiance to and reliance upon God, and persevere with faith and courage.

Rascals everywhere love having the Obstaclés Manifesto as their constant reminder of their greatness, their extended hand when they've fallen.

The battle is real and Obstaclés is strong. With the Obstaclés Manifesto as your shield, you're sure to conquer.

Watch this video to learn more about the Obstaclés character: http://youtu.be/nl4LZSYCndQ.

www.ChrisBrady.com

Obstaclés Manifesto

18" x 24"

■ Poster   ■ Canvas

Resolved Manifesto

Written by Orrin Woodward, also a co-founder of the Life Leadership company, the Resolved Manifesto displays Orrin's thirteen principles found in his book, *Resolved: 13 Resolutions for Life.*

Orrin's inspiring book takes us back in time to recapture the essence of what made America great. At the same time, it challenges readers to step up and recapture those principles and begin living them today.

It is at once a book of resolutions to assist a person in forging himself a true leader, a textbook of instructions to serve as a guide in tackling life's toughest challenges, and lastly, fully inspirational in capturing the heart and soul of leaders who have lived and achieved using the principles in this book.

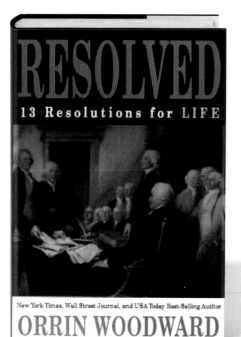

The Resolved Manifesto and book are both available for purchase at LifeManifestos.com. Purchase them together as a package deal to save 15 percent.

www.OrrinWoodward.com
www.Life-Leadership-Home.com

I RESOLVE...

to discover my God-given purpose.

to choose character over reputation any time they conflict.

to have a positive attitude in any situation.

to align my conscious (ant) mind with my
subconscious (elephant) mind towards my vision.

to develop and implement a
game plan in each area of my life.

to keep score in the game of life.

to develop the art and science of friendship.

to develop financial intelligence.

to develop the art and science of leadership.

to develop the art of conflict resolution.

to develop systems thinking.

to develop Adversity Quotient.

to reverse the current of decline in my field of mastery.

Resolved Manifesto

18" x 24"

ABOUT THE AUTHOR

 Stephen Palmer is an author, coach, and speaker devoted to helping people discover and liberate their greatness. He is the founder of Life Manifestos (LifeManifestos.com), and the author of *Uncommon Sense: A Common Citizen's Guide to Rebuilding America*.

He has a burning belief in the power of the human spirit—our ability to transcend circumstances and achieve greatness through choice. That belief drives him to strive for virtue and excellence in his own life, and to do all in his power to uplift and inspire others.

He co-authored, with Garrett Gunderson, the *New York Times*, *USA Today*, *Wall Street Journal*, *Businessweek*, and Amazon bestseller, *Killing Sacred Cows: Overcoming the Financial Myths that are Destroying Your Prosperity*. He also co-authored, with Kris Krohn, *The Conscious Creator: Six Laws for Manifesting Your Masterpiece Life*, as well as *Hub Mentality: Shifting from Business Transactions to Community Interaction* with Carl Woolston.

Stephen and his wife, Karina, are raising their four children in southern Utah. When he's not writing or spending time with his family, you'll find him reading, canyoneering in Zion National Park, gardening, or playing basketball.

Learn more about Stephen and subscribe to his popular "Inspiration Weekly" newsletter at StephenDPalmer.com.

SUBSCRIBE TO "INSPIRATION WEEKLY," THE FREE NEWSLETTER FOR PEOPLE WHO LIVE WITH PASSION & PURPOSE

Relish Exclusive, Life-Changing Insights from New York Times Bestselling Author Stephen Palmer Every Monday Morning

If you enjoy this book, you'll want to get every newsletter from Stephen Palmer.

Subscribe at StephenDPalmer.com to get thought-provoking content that inspires you to live with purpose, excellence, and significance. You'll love the weekly reminder to always strive for improvement. To follow your bliss. To make a difference. And your week won't be the same without it.

Unsolicited Praise for Inspiration Weekly:

"Stephen, YOU ARE A MARVEL! Thank you for your courage and passion. Thank you for choosing your own path and striving. Our family finds your writings and example very powerful and inspiring."

–Jenny Hanson

"Every Sunday night I wait up until the clock strikes midnight, so that I can read your latest newsletter. Thank you for always making me think, calm my fears, and reset my compass."

–Jonelle Hughes

"Just wanted to thank you for your inspiration weekly! It always uplifts me. Thank you for living your mission so that people like me can be strengthened and encouraged to live ours."

–Taylene Halverson

"Stephen, thank you for your words of wisdom and encouragement. Each week, I am inspired and challenged by what you have written. You are truly a gifted author."

–Ryan Sparks

"I cannot thank you enough for the inspiration and constant reminders that freedom loving people are alive and well."

–Jarad Rock

"Thanks for your constant inspiration. I read your articles to my children...even my 6 year old. The things you write about are, to me, some of the most important things we can teach our children. Keep up the good work. You are changing lives."

–Barbara Finlinson

Subscribe now at StephenDPalmer.com